Praise for
FOR LIF

'As strong and as light as a bird, *For Life* is a loving, courageous account of the black mess of grief and the slow return to a flourishing life. Perhaps it's only by staring death in the face that one can wholeheartedly celebrate the profound, joyful luck of being alive, and this book does both. Unflinching and tender, it shows us how to grieve. And it enacts the deep, human need to properly lay the dead to rest. You will cry reading this book, but you will also look up and see the world afresh, newly aware of the pulsing beat of your heart, grateful for the sun in your eyes.'

CHARLOTTE WOOD,
author of *Stone Yard Devotional*

'A beautiful, courageous and unflinching testament to life. To love shadowed by loss. To the howl of impermanence salved by beauty and the interconnectedness of all things. A book of hope and humanity.'

SARAH WINMAN,
author of *Still Life*

'The bigger the love, the greater the grief, the better the art. This beautiful book made my heart sing and break at the same time.'

MICHAEL ROBOTHAM,
author of *Storm Child*

'*For Life* is for everyone, for we all have—at some point in our lives— to deal with the loss of loved ones, and Ailsa Piper provides an intimate, clear-eyed account of her own journey. Imbued with a special sensitivity to the natural world, whether observing tiny, fragile-looking seahorses or magnificent birds in flight, this is a wondrous, delicately constructed memoir. I loved it.'

BILL HAYES,
author of *Insomniac City: New York, Oliver Sacks, and Me*

'Ailsa Piper's superpower is noticing, paying meticulous attention to the exquisite minutiae of daily life—the gifted writer's greatest tool. In this raw yet delicate memoir, Ailsa's poetic sensibilities elevate these small things—seahorses, birds in flight, flowers, the little still lifeş she curates around her home, the foibles and nobility of her fellow humans—to art. There is wisdom and poetry and a sense of the sacred here in her rich evocations of her father's poignant final chapter, a rendering of Covid lockdowns that almost makes one nostalgic for its deprivations and oddities, her ardent love and heart-wrenching grief for a life partner gone too soon, whom we come to love too. She casts a spell that leaves the reader incapable of un-noticing the truth: that life is speaking to us in every moment. *For Life* evokes stillness, clarity, appreciation. It left me more attentive to life, its beauty and challenges, my own idiosyncrasies, the delicacy of love. What a gift.'

TIM BAKER,
author of *Patting the Shark*

'Ailsa Piper has exquisitely wrought words and sentences into an intoxicating experience of life, love, loss and beauty. This is a courageous, vulnerable and joyful work that lingers long after the pages are turned. Tender, strong, and sensitively drawn from a life led in wonder, curiosity, loss, joy and wisdom, Piper's writing makes you want to dance, sing, soar, be held and be free. I was filled with an urge to both dive into the ocean, and to breathe in the world deeply. *For Life* proves Piper to be a poet and modern seer.'

SUZIE MILLER,
author of *Prima Facie*

'A love letter to the past, present and future, and a beautiful demonstration of one true path to immortality—through memory and sharing story. Ailsa Piper's *For Life* sits with the idea of honouring both death and life, the realities of reconciliation and improvisation, and the sacredness of the right words to hold the right moments. It's a powerful meditation on gratitude and what Piper describes as "respectful lives of decency and kindness"—all of which combine to make a buoying and restorative kind of love.'

ASHLEY HAY,
author of *A Hundred Small Lessons*

'In this exploration—fossick, ramble, dance, even romp—in search of good ways to live on alone after losing a husband whose loss has laid waste to her, Ailsa Piper's many-sided humanity flowers and shines. It is not a dark book—it is a cornflower-blue and sun-filled book, looking death, which is always hovering, straight in the eye.'

ROBERT DESSAIX,
author of *What Days Are For*

'A deeply companionable read. Quiet, profound and full of wonderment.'

HANNIE RAYSON,
author of *Hello Beautiful*

'If it takes a community to raise a child, Ailsa Piper shows us that it also takes a community to draw a person away from the tilting world of sudden grief to find a new accommodation with life. One beat-perfect scene made me gasp with the hard question it asks and the even gutsier answer it provides. Filled with Piper's characteristic warmth and intelligence, *For Life* is also a superbly drawn portrait of a place and the precious everyday doings of the natural world. A beautifully put-together story told with skill, candour—and love.'

VICKI HASTRICH,
author of *Night Fishing*

'Tender and wise. A story about loss that shines with life, like the shattered sea glass Piper collects on Sydney shores . . .'

KRISTINA OLSSON,
author of *Shell*

'Both intimate and sweeping, *For Life* honours the everyday, the ordinary, in all its holiness. Like the still lifes Ailsa Piper writes about, her brilliant pages are still lifes too, and in them readers will find love and grief, language and longing, heartache and flight. Through conversations with her beloved, and careful observations of joy and pain, Piper brings us close—to her loss, to this life, to the world. *For Life* is a love letter. Readers will want to carry it with them.'

SARAH SENTILLES,
author of *Draw Your Weapons*

AILSA PIPER's first book was the travel memoir *Sinning Across Spain*. Then came *The Attachment: Letters from a most unlikely friendship*, which was co-authored with Tony Doherty. She has written for radio and theatre, and her script *Small Mercies* was co-winner of the Patrick White Playwright's Award. Ailsa also worked as an actor and director for many years and is an accomplished audiobook narrator.

FOR LIFE

A memoir of living and dying—and flying

AILSA PIPER

ALLEN&UNWIN

SYDNEY • MELBOURNE • AUCKLAND • LONDON

Fragments of this work were first published in *Water's Edge: Writing on
water*, edited by Lenore Manderson and Forrest Gander. Copyright © 2023
by Northwestern University Press. All rights reserved.

Allen & Unwin
Cammeraygal Country
83 Alexander Street
Crows Nest NSW 2065
Australia
Phone: (61 2) 8425 0100
Email: info@allenandunwin.com
Web: www.allenandunwin.com

*Allen & Unwin acknowledges the Traditional Owners of the Country
on which we live and work. We pay our respects to all Aboriginal and
Torres Strait Islander Elders, past and present.*

 A catalogue record for this
book is available from the
National Library of Australia

ISBN 978 1 76147 086 8

Set in 11/20 pt Minion Pro by Bookhouse, Sydney
Printed and bound in Australia by the Opus Group

10 9 8 7 6 5 4 3 2 1

The paper in this book is FSC® certified.
FSC® promotes environmentally responsible,
socially beneficial and economically viable
management of the world's forests.

FOR ALANNA

To live is so startling, it leaves but little room for other occupations . . .

EMILY DICKINSON

CONTENTS

Before . . .

RANGER JOHN'S VOICE rises above the squabble of seagulls.

'Wriggle if you want to live.'

On cue, the seahorse unfurls. Caught in autumn sunlight, he's a restless brown lifeline in my palm, his knobbly exoskeleton surprisingly hard. He headbutts me once, twice, but his attack is only a tickle on my salty skin.

John and his team shuffle across the sand, mindful of their steps as they squint into an enormous kelp-encrusted net, searching for any other seahorses that might have used it to make their unlikely homes. The curly creatures must be relocated so that any frayed fibres can be repaired. After all, the net's main purpose is to protect humans. The official name of this curve of water, where I swim each morning, is Shark Beach.

(Notice that, Pete? So casual . . . *where I swim each morning* . . .)

The gulls hover, greedy opportunists on the lookout for any wriggler that could be brunch. There are perils aplenty for seahorses, and the loss of native habitat—grass beds and algae—has led to this local species being declared endangered.

With my right hand, I shade the mini-stallion as he wriggles again. 'It's okay,' I whisper. 'I'm here. I've got you.'

Almost a thousand kilometres south, on the thirty-fifth floor of a city high-rise in Melbourne, another unlikely home awaits its tenants. Soon, a pair of feathered predators with hooked beaks and high-vis claws will arrive. They will land on a narrow concrete ledge in the clouds to lay their eggs and raise this year's chicks. For decades they've come, despite the implications of their name.

Peregrine, I found in an online dictionary. *Having a tendency to wander.*

(And yes, Pete, I should have consulted a real dictionary—but even so, that definition could have been written just for me.)

These peregrine falcons might wander for the rest of the year, but in autumn they come home—and like the seahorses, they've chosen a man-made place. Protected only by a bank of metal louvres, the falcons will settle onto their urban 'scrape' to nest under the gaze of a streaming webcam. Thanks to its all-seeing eye, I'll observe this year's hatchlings become fledglings, eavesdropping on their first tentative tweets and, later, their insistent shrieks for food. My avian pilgrims care nothing for lockdowns or borders. They will return, and I will watch, envious of their certainty about where they belong.

'Come on,' Ranger John calls again. 'Wriggle.'

I landed here in Sydney six years ago in a welter of pain, panic and instinct. I'd been in fight-or-flight mode for twelve months, longing to feel safe enough to stop but driven to keep flying. I brought almost nothing of my previous life. Grief had made me ruthless; I threw and threw.

(And yes, I do know how appalled you'd have been by that, Pete.)

My father implored me to wait; to cling to the familiar. Constants, he advised, would give me scaffolding. Decades ago, when his second wife, my stepmother, died in bed beside him, habits were his protection and comfort—along with a daily packet or two of cigarettes.

My drug of choice was movement. Dad couldn't get through to me, and neither could friends who urged me to slow, to keep, to stay in Melbourne, in my home. Instead, I fled, to this *harbour* . . .

A place of shelter or refuge.

Around its shore, rangers have installed seahorse 'hotels'—mesh boxes tethered at locations they've identified as safe—but this shark net has long been a favoured seahorse squat. The annual ritual of hauling in sections of it in a dinghy, laying them on the sand and then searching for wriggling residents, marks the end of the summer swim season. It's my favourite day of the year—although I haven't lived here long enough to make such an extravagant claim.

'Come on, you know the drill,' Ranger John calls. 'Wriggle to live.'

My new friend squirms.

I scan the sky, half-expecting a flurry of grey feathers. A peregrine falcon would gulp down a seahorse as an amuse-bouche before murdering a silver gull for mains.

Peregrina.

That's what the locals called me in Spain. All along the trails I'd hear it. *Hola, peregrina.* Hello, pilgrim.

I've walked thousands of kilometres of roads—or *caminos*—across that seductive land, often under power lines where storks had constructed massive nests in which to raise their pointy-billed chicks. I've followed cuckoo calls along solo trails in Italy, France and Portugal, sometimes wondering if I were cuckoo myself. I've hiked in the Central Desert of Australia, where flocks of budgerigars stained the sky green and gold; and in the unpredictable Tasmanian uplands, where crafty crows undo backpacks in a trice, stealing all the snacks.

Walking is where I can best be with my self. The rhythm of plodding is familiar and restorative. Even on uncertain ground, I feel peaceful and, yes, home. Maybe that's why movement seems like the answer when fears rise.

In Spain, where I was called *peregrina*, it would never have occurred to me that I had anything in common with birds of prey, yet just like the peregrines returning to their urban eyrie, back then I too had a homing impulse towards Melbourne, and my true north. My internal compass was set to him; the fixed point in my cosmos.

Peter.

The name comes from ancient Greek. It means *rock*. In all dictionaries.

Hippocampus.

That word also comes from Greek. *Hippos* means *horse*. *Kampos* means *sea monster*. This one's glossy belly looks fit to burst. Carrying babies—called *fry*—is the job of the male, and a pregnancy lasts about three weeks. My mini-monster has a pouch in which his mate has laid hundreds of eggs. I snuggle my toes, replicas of my father's, into the cool sand and observe my fertile friend as he curls and uncurls in my hand, which could be my mother's, right down to the shape of the nail beds.

Ranger John says our little guy is a White's Seahorse. The species is unique, in that couples are monogamous their whole lives—up to six years. Peregrine falcons also mate for life. For them, that could be almost twenty years. Peter and I had nearly twenty-eight.

Seahorses are the world's slowest-moving fish. In fact, John says, you could say they flutter rather than swim, at about two metres per hour. I should tell him that peregrines are the fastest creatures in the animal kingdom and can dive at almost

350 kilometres per hour, but I'm distracted by his description of the way seahorses dance when they're courting. He can't know how that pleases me. I associate dancing with Peter's and my beginnings—though, as with the seahorses, a more accurate word for what I'm remembering might be mating.

John describes how seahorses hold each other's tails as they tango, and even change colour from neutral dun to sunny yellow or cream. They're enticing images, but the wriggling in my palm must surely be distress at the loss of his home and partner. Do I have a handful of grief? I'm too embarrassed to ask John, who has just recorded the length of my sinewy friend's spine, but the seemingly prosaic ranger surprises me as he turns back to the net.

'Seahorses drew Poseidon's chariot,' he calls to me. 'They're tougher than you think.'

The sea god must have been a lightweight, because this wriggler weighs no more than a twig. Perhaps Poseidon commanded a whole navy of hippocampi.

(I know. Such a lovely plural, Pete.)

All mammals have two hippocampi. They're located on either side of our brains. Ridges of grey matter shaped like seahorses, they help us to hold on to memories, to arrange and file them, and to form new ones. They connect places and emotions; without them, we might never be able to find our way, or recognise our home when we reach it. If our cerebral seahorses are hurt, we risk losing parts of ourselves in the dark waters of forgetfulness.

Our hippocampi can also grow in volume when we learn a new language. I like to remind myself of that when I trip or stumble in another tongue.

On a *chemin* in France, where the word *peregrina* translated into *pèlerine*, a local dressed all in black told me a female pilgrim had been found in the Pyrenees, after the vultures had finished with her. Ah yes, she was a lone hiker just like you, the old woman said with Gallic relish, but she'd been reduced to bones and clothes and a mutilated backpack.

'*Non. C'est terrible,*' I gasped, recalling two griffon vultures I'd seen the previous day, ripping open the stomach of a sheep, removing gizzards as efficiently as the men I'd watched slaughtering creatures for meat when I was a kid. Those birds, beaks deep in bloody flesh, barely acknowledged me.

Oh, don't you worry, the Gallic crone continued; that silly *pèlerine* had fallen down the side of the mountain first. She was already dead when the *vautours* got to her.

For miles afterwards I scanned the sky, fearful I might spot a winged attacker, yet every winter I wait impatiently for the arrival of the peregrines. I, who can't stomach a horror movie, will stare into my computer screen as a mother falcon tears at the flesh of its kill.

I have a bank of memories of the falcons—some tender, some funny, some ferocious; many shared with Peter. Before technology allowed their nest to be streamed to the world, we would make forays into the city to observe the peregrines on a screen in the foyer of their high-rise. We'd huddle with other fans, transfixed by the antics thirty-five floors above. It was the best show in town. Standing room only. Now, the webcam lets me add to my memory bank, even from afar.

That makes it sound like my recollections are ordered and orderly, but my hippocampi have proven themselves unreliable plenty of times. Still, what can you expect from a creature that changes colour when it tangos?

Lately, I find myself clutching at memories like a falcon seizing a sparrow. Making sense of them is hard. Are they real or reconstructed from stories? I ask my ninety-year-old father, who is 3962 kilometres west, as the crow flies, in Perth.

Dad jokes about forgetting the important things, but he retrieves much that is intriguing. In this, he is still the parent bird seeking nourishment for his chick. We talk by phone because I can't travel to him; his state border is closed in response to Covid. Perth is the most geographically isolated city in the world, and now it is further sequestered. For six months I've been trying and failing to get permission to see him, so I have become adept at reading his tones and pauses in our daily call. I've learned to wait while he fights for breath, trying to gauge by his coughs, inhalations and throat-clearings whether it's a good or bad day.

He can neither confirm nor deny many of my memories, but still I persist, like a toddler relentlessly demanding *why*? Is that true, Dad? Did this happen, in this way? He chuckles, then gasps, exhales and changes position, wriggling for life. In the background, a crow calls.

Aaaaark.

Eventually, Dad speaks again. 'Memory doesn't always match up with the truth, honey. You should know that—the daughter of divorced parents.'

We both laugh, but I know how significant that long-ago break-up remains for him. In the early sixties, divorce meant a loss of respectability. Middle-class judgement came like an attack from above, vicious and swift.

Dad insists he's lucky, and yet it's the last adjective I would apply to him. His mother was killed, mown down by a speeding driver along with her sister, when he was twenty-nine. His father, a war veteran who had been gassed, never recovered from her loss. Five years later, and after only six years of marriage, my mother left Dad. His second wife died of an aneurysm, in their bed, when he was in his fifties. He has never had financial security, either, yet he endlessly asserts his good fortune, and his favourite song is 'What a Wonderful World'. His characterisation of himself as The Lucky Man may have been his salvation.

I hear the thin rasps of air, in and out.

'Sorry, honey,' he manages to say. 'I'm fine. Don't you worry.'

The conversation has cost him, and as I wait, holding my breath, I understand that I'm still just a kid in his eyes. I'm 'daughter' before walker or writer or widow, and I always will be, no matter how frail he becomes. And part of me reverts to daughter when I'm with him, for better and, sometimes, for snappish worse.

But memories?

I don't know which ones to trust—and Dad is a bank I can't access at will anymore. There are places he does not wish to revisit, and people with whom his hippocampus needs to linger. Maybe there are ghosts to be laid to rest. His focus is fixed on what is vital to him. Mine is haphazard and blurred. I need the eyes of a peregrine.

The seahorse's tail twists upwards. His neck arches, bobbing in time to some rhythm from the deep. Perhaps he's remembering his mate. Maybe these twists are involuntary courting moves, random recollections making him sashay in the sunshine.

Will this forced removal from his home affect those memories, in the way that Alzheimer's patients can be disrupted when they're moved into care? Dad is now so physically debilitated that he can barely walk more than a dozen paces without a 'breather', but his mind is razor-sharp, and his greatest fear is of being uprooted from his modest unit. 'I just want to stay put,' he says. 'I know who I am here at home.'

It's a big claim, and one I can't make with any confidence. When I uprooted from Melbourne, did I lose pieces of myself?

Maybe I wanted to reclaim a self that was not part of Peter—but can there be such a self? After all, my identity was entwined with his for almost all my adult life.

Ranger John returns with kelp fronds for the white bucket, so I take the opportunity to ask whether my seahorse will recall his home on the net. Or, I ask, is 'home' located in the presence of that other, the one with whom he joined tails for life? Perhaps home is not a place, I say, but a familiar curved spine. John just grins and calls me a seahorse-whisperer.

An osprey circles, casting a moving V-shaped shadow.

V for vulture.

I lean forward to shield the pregnant patriarch from view, just as he arches, seemingly aware of the threat from the skies. I don't want to farewell him, but it's time. He has been too long in the air. I head for the white bucket, where three others wait for him in their temporary digs. I hope one of them might be his mate; that they will clasp tails and dance in celebration.

I take one final mental snapshot so I can describe him to Dad. Then I slide my hand into the water and my curly friend is off, propelling himself around his new environs, wriggling for life.

Still life with dictionary

AN APPLE CORE, browning at the edges, sat on the tatty cover of a French grammar textbook. Beside it, dregs of milky tea had coagulated in the bottom of a chunky ceramic mug. Nearby, a well-thumbed edition of the *Oxford English Reference Dictionary* lay open at page 485, where a word—*eustasy*—was marked in black pen with a tick and two squiggly brackets beside it.

That still life on our scratched wooden coffee table told of a ritual I'd observed for decades. Every day, Peter completed thirty minutes of language study: lists of vocab, snippets of slang from subtitled TV dramas and the obligatory repetition of verbs. His hippocampi were given plenty of chances to expand. If I'd opened that French grammar book—*Easy to read, easy to use, easy to understand*—I'd have seen scrawls, translations and queries, corners turned down and subjunctives circled.

Every day, he'd also read five pages of his reference dictionary. This one had been a birthday present from his sister and her family ten years earlier. No gift ever gave so much. Words would be underlined or starred if they had special significance. Some would be transcribed onto the backs of used envelopes, so he could revise on the run. Often, there'd be an entry that had to be discussed with me; a discovery so intriguing it must be shared. *Eustasy* was not one of those. I'd never seen it before.

The dictionary ritual was Peter in flâneur mode. That was how he identified himself—he even had it printed on his business cards: *Actor and flâneur*—using the French word for someone who wanders without destination, roving haphazardly in search of the overlooked thing. That was his way of walking, but it was also his way of reading: curious yet relaxed; unwilling to be rushed; pottering around corners or down alleys, sniffing out random astonishments.

Another ritual: he would eat a piece of fruit as he sipped tea.

'They don't go together,' I'd say, as he chomped into an apple or banana and grinned at me over the rim of his favourite mug.

Now, I wonder how many times we asked each other that one-word question—'Tea?'—before flicking the switch on the kettle.

Five times a day?

That would be a conservative estimate. We were together for twenty-seven years and eight months. So let's say 10,095 days.

Multiplied by five, that's 50,475 times. No wonder we had to bleach favourite cups to remove tannin stains.

I shivered.

Insipid light filtered into the room, stippling the still life. It was easy to decipher, easy to 'read', but I could not—or would not—understand what it was telling me. I focused on the dictionary; those annotations on page 485. Why the tick and the brackets? What was so important about that particular word?

eustasy
a change in sea level throughout the world caused by tectonic movements, melting of glaciers etc.

This made some sense. We were both concerned about the climate emergency and furious at the inaction of leaders. Peter fretted about the loss of Indonesian rainforests and orangutans; he grieved for the sea turtles that mistook plastic bags for jellyfish, filling their stomachs on waste and so starving to death. He constructed placards to hold at rallies and devised punning protest signs for his car's rear window. On election days, he would sit at the local polling booth, asking voters to consider which party had the most effective policies on emissions and sustainability. (Amazingly, these encounters were mostly civil, even in disagreement.) His life's dream was to visit Antarctica, a place of mythic perfection for him.

Despite his fair skin, so prone to sunburn, he loved to

beachcomb. His preferred getaway was a week in a rented shack near a hamlet called Aireys Inlet, where there was a red-capped white lighthouse and kilometres of coast for foraging. He'd holidayed there with his parents and sisters when he was a kid, and often talked of lazy days spent with another family who had a boy about his age. They would paddle a tinnie across the lagoon or fossick for hours in the dunes. Sometimes they raced each other around the top of the lighthouse, circling in the sky. But he was never a boardrider, preferring the thump of his chest against sand at the end of a bodysurf, and he was aghast that I'd never learned freestyle.

'Call yourself Australian?' he'd tease, as I lingered in the shallows, alert for dark shapes and dorsal fins.

Maybe he'd intended to tell me about *eustasy* when we next spoke on the phone. I imagined him playing with its syllables as a way of remembering it. He'd do that sometimes when he was memorising lines for a role.

Eustasy. Eusta-sea. Used-to-see . . .

We used to see stable sea levels, but eustasy has altered that.

Language was one of the chief pleasures of a new script. He was diligent in the hunt for clues to a character, playful with possibilities for accents or physicality, and devoted to the craft of his work. It's fair to say the theatre was his first love. I learned early on to step aside in deference to it, and rarely minded. After all, I'd fallen for him on stage long before I met him.

———

The dictionary's column of *eu* entries continued.

eutectic

Euterpe

euthanasia

They were waiting to be graded for interest, but the adjudicator was gone. A tectonic movement had occurred.

I flicked forward to page 632, locating the three-syllable word that kept drumming in my head.

haemorrhage

1. *an escape of blood from a ruptured blood vessel, esp. when profuse*

It happened on Sunday, 18 May 2014.

Time unknown.

It was just another week in our lives.

No. That's not entirely accurate.

On the previous Sunday night, Peter had shown me a list of jobs that needed to be done in order to sell our cedar shack in the country, and another list of repairs that would make it possible to rent or sell our weatherboard cottage in town. I laughed and said we couldn't have both places on the market at the same time. Where would we live?

He laughed right back at me. 'When did you get to be such a worrier? You've kipped in plenty of refuges and hostels.'

We went to sleep, both of us dreaming of change. That was what was unusual. Normally, I was the one agitating for reinvention. Like Dad, Peter preferred continuity—one of the weapons he used against his internal demons was constancy. Those lists were the result of months of him asking hard questions of himself, confronting long-held memories and fears. He was intending to relinquish more than real estate.

On Monday, he dropped me at the airport, telling me to give our old friend Amanda a hug when I got to Sydney. Unusually, I was reluctant to leave, huddling against his chest.

'Go on,' he said. 'Go quickly so you can come back quickly.'

I turned away, then turned back, following him to his car in its two-minute park.

He laughed. 'Go on, now. You know I love you.'

Of course I knew. After more than twenty-seven years, I knew it in every cell, even the ones that contained the tests and demands of a long relationship. Perhaps I knew it more keenly in those. What I didn't know was that a predator was hovering.

He kissed me, then set off to the shack, already anticipating the pleasure of autumn burning and the phone call to the estate agent. He had plans.

In the following days, he was upbeat, texting photos of yellow leaves on the oaks at the General Store, and on Wednesday, back in the city, news that he'd completed his circuit of the

Botanic Gardens in record time. We talked that night. I'd gone shopping with Amanda, I reported. My work gig had been a success and I felt sure my glandular fever was on the way out. He was preparing for his role on a new TV series—I'd filmed his screen test. I could hear him blowing on his soup. It was the minestrone I'd made before leaving.

Thursday's photo showed his post-run training food—a white chocolate muffin—and on Friday night we texted back and forth. He was intending to go up country the next day for more burning.

On Saturday, I went to seek out a grave at the big cemetery overlooking the Pacific Ocean. This was research for a book I was writing. Roaming across the undulating acres of the dead, I felt excitement and possibility. I saw no portents, only shorebirds wheeling. Even the raven on the stone angel's shoulder, silhouetted against sun and sea, seemed merely picturesque, as though two feathered friends had colluded for a photo op.

On Sunday, Amanda cooked a roast, and afterwards I tried to call Peter.

He didn't answer.

I wasn't concerned. Truth be told, I was a bit irritated. Often, he didn't hear the faint bleat of his ancient Nokia, and he frequently didn't take it with him if he went out. I'd hassled him about upgrading it but that was not his style. He was a keeper.

Maybe he was still in the bush, burning off or raking, grappling with gorse and cursing whoever introduced it to Australia. Amanda agreed—he would have worked until the last light faded.

I tried him again.

Still no answer.

Where are you, Pete?

I called the hated mobile at shorter and shorter intervals, even though he certainly wouldn't have picked up if he'd been on the freeway, driving back to town.

Peter, where are you?

It was dark. He should be home by now. Amanda was watching *Call the Midwife* in the next room as I stabbed at the telephone. Calling . . .

Where is Peter?

Calling again.

Where is he?

Finally, I rang our neighbour, a doctor, and asked him to use his key to go into our home. It was after 10 p.m. by then. When he phoned back, he said five words.

'Oh, Ailsa. I'm so sorry.'

Later, I would want to ask Peter whether 'oh' was a word. He was the one person who would think it a reasonable question.

Later still, my GP would try to reassure me that I wouldn't have been able to keep him alive if I'd been with him.

'It would have been like a hammer to the back of the head,' she said. 'Excruciating for a second, then nothing.'

Later again, our doctor neighbour would tell me he searched the house that night but found no note. At the time, I couldn't understand why he would say such a thing, because almost no one knew about Peter's intermittent struggles with depression, but perhaps he was just looking for a reason. I certainly wanted one. I wanted an explanation. I wanted someone, anyone, a medical specialist, a god or some winged thing with sharp eyes and grasping talons, to take responsibility, but everyone said the same thing. It could not have been foreseen. This was random, they said. Just terrible bad luck.

Luck. That single-syllable shyster of a word, so dear to my father.

I didn't buy it. Peter died alone, in the bed we'd bought fifteen years earlier, in the bedroom we'd shared for almost twenty-eight years. He was taken, alone, to lie in the *morgue*. That was a word whose bizarre French origins we had discussed, years before, while standing on a bridge in Paris; but in the anguished darkness of the previous night as Amanda's little dog circled from her to me and back again, and on the interminable flight to Melbourne that morning, and in the dread silence of the present, and for the excoriating days to come, the word kept reverberating, flashing up images of him, cold and alone on a concrete slab, just like the grey ledge where the peregrine falcons nested.

Someone had to be accountable for Peter's death, and if no one else was to blame, then the fault must be mine. I had left my station. It was negligence.

'You do know you don't keep planes in the air, don't you?' a friend joked, weeks later. I laughed with her, but inside I knew. His death was on me.

haemorrhage

(Another word that comes from the Greek, Pete.) *haima* = blood and *rhegnumi* = burst: a bloodburst.

2. *an extensive damaging loss suffered by a state, organization etc., esp. of people or assets*

Loss.

Of husband, friend, champion.

Of purpose, way, marbles and meaning. Of self. Of home.

Loss.

Extensive and damaging.

I'M NOT AWARE the rain is falling until I inhale. Droplets hit the surface then bounce up again, backlit against dawn light. For an instant, the harbour and heavens are connected via thin strands of liquid. On each head turn, raindrops rebound, pirouetting one last time before dissolving, like me, into the tidal sway.

I stroke away the thought that recurs like a heartbeat: how Peter would love it, and how he would marvel at me, in it. (Seven years on, Pete. Seven years. Where might you be? Can you *be* anything now?)

I stroke away the other thought: that I'm swimming through Peter; that when he was cremated and his atoms went into the ether, some of them could have come here, could be around me anywhere, even in the water, stroking me.

Inhale. Slow. Exhale. Slow . . .

I flip and float, letting the downpour splash onto my face as a colder current swirls around my toes. Rivulets form on my goggles. I'm a still thing between universes of movement. Clouds bump and glide, morphing from steel through dove to the pearliest of greys. This day will be soft—dull, even. That will please my mermaid friend. She maintains colours are more intense when the sun hides away.

Marina is the most aptly named person I know. We've swum together on many mornings: rain, shine or bluster. A childhood champion in the pool, she insists she doesn't have feet but flippers. Out of the water, she's an artist, working in oils and inks to make landscapes and portraits. She also paints still lifes (another plural I like, Pete) of flowers in shapely vases: grevilleas, camellias, callistemons, daisies and dahlias.

One day, at the water's edge, we got talking to one of the regular swimmers. A perennially curious octogenarian, the Old Salt asked Marina how artists paint light. She replied that she doesn't paint it because we don't actually see it. Rather, we see its effect on the things it touches.

'A bit like love,' he said, limping away across the sand, leaving us in open-mouthed silence. Everyone's a philosopher, here on the shore.

A seagull flaps once, then cruises across my field of vision, coordinating with sky and clouds. A murder of crows—or is it a conspiracy of ravens?—wings along behind it. They are black-beaked seraphim, heralding the day.

Aaar. Aaar. Aaaark.

Beyond the remaining section of shark net—left there so the seahorses can continue to make homes—a crew of rowers is in training. The reedy squawks of their guide slice the moist air.

Stroke. Stroke.

He and the crows make a counterpointing cacophony.

Stroke. Aaaark. Stroke. Aaaark.

The world's largest living creature, the blue whale, can hear other whales from a thousand kilometres away. Seahorses may not hear from such distances, but they do communicate with each other by faint sounds that we can't discern. If they're registering the boy's high-pitched urging from their home down on the net, would they recognise it as human?

Stroke.

Droplets converge, trickling over my breastbone like fingers. *Stroke.* I shiver, but I'm not cold. My edges dissolve and blur, melding with the brine. *Stroke.* I open, legs and arms wide. I'm all here and all now, as though my hippocampi have taken the day off, and are content just to loll in a liquid present.

Aaaaark!

Crows are not sensualists. They're super smart, but their voices could never be called seductive. I shut out their squawks and focus on the other end of the beach, where an apple-green swimsuit has caught my attention. Its wearer thought she'd never swim again, but she's back, pushed in a wheelchair to the edge of the concrete stairs. She rises, gripping onto her son, and does a bandy-legged crabwalk across the sand. Once the water reaches her thighs, she lets go, free to float as her son completes his laps.

'He's a good egg,' she told me last week, and her fifty-year-old captain-of-industry boy ducked his head, blushing, before swimming away from us.

I freestyle west, towards the sandstone headland, which has paled from granite to shale grey. Most mornings, I stroke between the almost-pink sky of sunrise and the warm gold of those pitted rocks, but now the world is the colour of a tern's wing, like the one I glimpse as I rotate my head to breathe.

My hands cleave through a school of darting streaks, tiny fish whose name I still don't know. Behind them, a yellowtail scad curves while two sand whiting cruise. There's so much movement in this glittering underworld; so much flickering life. The Old Salt claims that over eighty per cent of all living things are found in the ocean, and it does feel that way, despite Ranger John's insistence on declining numbers. I prefer the 'evidence' of my newcomer's eyes. To me, the life beneath is startling.

Down here, there's no virus. Bobbing up to locate ourselves, we inhale free of fear before submerging again. On the sand, we towel off at arm's distance, just as we used to march into class at primary school, checking our positions by reaching out to the shoulders of the person ahead.

That's my own memory; not from a photograph or story. I can see my fingertips touching the brown-and-white cotton check of Robin's uniform.

Robin. Name of a bird. Dancing Robin, bobbin' robin, always ahead by a step; dead of cancer at seventeen. After her leg was amputated, she would still go to the water, held up by friends until the Indian Ocean could support her. What would she have made of Covid? What would you make of it, Pete, this airborne predator whose name is not in your dictionary? It's like the sea lice that sting my flesh. I only know I've met them when they're inside my swimming togs, feasting, or nipping along my chest and calves. And it's on the move again, they say. It's called Delta now, and already it seems likely to make it impossible to fly west for Dad's ninety-first birthday. I missed his ninetieth last year, thanks to the virus.

Border closures. Who would have thought, Pete? And who could have foreseen that we'd become numb to a word like 'unprecedented'? Along with 'awesome', it has been rendered almost meaningless.

No, that's not true. Under the surface, there is still awe. Last week, I lashed out on fancy goggles so I could observe the flick of a leatherjacket's tail or the whisk of a toadfish along the creamy sand floor. I'm dazzled by the splashy strangeness of it all. I'll need decades to be able to claim comprehension of this underworld. I pray the watery gods will grant me time.

———

After Peter died—seven years and one month ago—even walking couldn't settle my hypervigilant heart. His death laid waste to the 'me' that had been. In fact, I had no idea if there even was a 'me' without him. I looked at everything, all our belongings, our home, with changed eyes, trying to see if they could show me who we had been together, and who I was to be now.

Eventually, when I couldn't find answers or solace, the observing turned into discarding. Almost everything went, including his two ancient cars, the bush shack that we'd bought twenty-five years earlier, and our cottage in the city, which he'd had before we met. Contents of both places were donated, trashed or sold. I kept some paintings and a couple of small tables he had given me. I kept kitchen utensils and crockery. I kept his cloth-bound Shakespeare, and the photo of him playing Hamlet, taken twenty years before we met.

... *there's a special providence in the fall of a sparrow*, the Danish prince said, but what if the sparrow is plucked from above?

Hamlet also claimed *the readiness is all*. I raged that Peter had been taken unready and too soon.

When the remaining flotsam and jetsam of our life together was packed into the front third of a small removal truck, I drove up the highway to Sydney, back to Amanda's spare room. It was a haven, but it was also the place where Peter had died—where I had heard our neighbour's voice, nine months earlier.

'Oh, Ailsa . . .'

Every night, those words reverberated against the sage green walls and wooden shutters. No amount of reassurance from Amanda could silence them. When I closed my eyes, I'd see her at the bedroom door, watching as I spoke to our neighbour in Melbourne, then backing away, saying, 'No, no.' Over and over. 'No. Oh no.' Before I had uttered a sound, she had seen something, and she knew.

My hippocampi stored those images, dancing around them endlessly. If only my cerebral seahorses could conjure up the history I threw into a rubbish skip. There was a cardboard box containing all my diaries, as far back as 1978—long before the internet or synchronised calendars. They were not journals, but a meticulous record of dailiness: workouts and medical appointments, voice jobs and lunches, language classes and theatre outings. Every hour accounted for and colour-coded. I'd grabbed the box and flung it onto the seat of a broken-backed chair.

I thought, then, that I would never want to look back, but now that box is the one thing I regret tossing. Decades, gone. So much of my memory bank went with Peter; so much had gone already with Mum. No wonder I pester Dad now.

With every night I spent in Amanda's guest room, I grew more fearful and less able to see a future. The need to find a place of my own, with no reverberations from Peter's loss, was urgent, and on days when there were no flats to view,

I despaired. So, I went to water. I'd walk down to the nearby ferry stop, board the first craft, and travel from jetty to jetty. Even though I was going nowhere, riding the boats made it seem I was progressing.

One morning, seated on the upper deck among a gaggle of commuters, I noticed my dress was inside out. I stood, whipped it over my head, turned it right way out, pulled it back on and sat down again. Besuited workers gawped, perhaps wondering why a middle-aged woman would perform a feeble striptease before breakfast. I couldn't have told them. I had no idea who or why I was.

Back at Amanda's, I would walk by the mangroves along the nearby creek, up to the village shops, back across grassy slopes, and down to the paperbark forest with its colony of flying foxes, but the underlying hum never stopped. Who was I to be, now? How was I to keep going?

One day, passing an outdoor swimming pool, I heard a woman instructing someone in the water.

There's plenty of air, she called. *Just breathe it in. Left then right. Breathe.*

Without stopping to talk myself out of it, I asked her to teach me to swim.

I grew up in the bush. Red dust, spinifex and bone-dry air were my familiars. I was a land creature; earthed. I never learned to swim because there was no water, except when a cyclone brought flooding, and by the time I came to my city school, it was easier to feign an interest in hurdles than to admit to ignorance, or to my fear of drowning. But after Peter died, I wanted to battle—mostly with myself. Maybe, I figured, conquering a forever terror would remind me that I could be brave enough, deserving enough, of more time on this blue planet.

That makes it sound like I knew what I was doing. I didn't. But I did get into the water.

Learning to swim was relearning to breathe. I was so sure I would go under—and maybe there was a part of me that wanted to, but my Amazon teacher was not having that. Water had always been fear-full, I explained to her: something to sweep you away. Water was where we dissolved. It was lost breath. It was death. Or, at least, the deep was . . .

I started at the shallow end, with a child's kickboard. *That's it. Kick kick kick.* I worked hard, urged on by my teacher until my toes couldn't touch the bottom. Then, fear pushed the air from my body and I would panic, salt tears mingling with chlorine as I held and held my breath.

But my teacher insisted I come back to the present, back to the pool, to the day. I had to roll my head to the side, she said, as though laying it on a pillow of water. *Now inhale*, she shouted, *fill yourself full, then roll back to look down at the stripe along the bottom, and exhale. Keep kicking and roll left.*

Over and over she worked to get me to breathe.

Suck the air in, deep into your belly, then roll right, then breathe out like there is time, all the time in the world . . .

That's what my Amazon chanted at the third lesson, and I wanted to explain that time was the thing we dare not assume; that the winged predator could seize us at any moment—here, now, anywhere—but talking underwater eluded even me, and so I breathed like I'd never breathed before, like my mother would never breathe again, rolling to inhale, stroking, making time, breathing like my father could only breathe in dreams, breathing in as I reached for the time that Peter no longer had, breathing them all in, breathing them all out . . .

The first time I swam in the harbour, where there were no edges or markings, I wouldn't lift my feet from the safety of sand. Finally, when I saw a toddler strike out with plump arms flailing, I was shamed into movement. I bounced up, lifting off as I gulped a lungful of air, and began to stroke like a cartoon character—even before I was immersed or horizontal.

Love wasn't instant; there was no immediate infatuation with salt water. It took time, and commitment, but always, after that, swimming began with the lift. It still does. Maybe it's what gulls feel as they take off, or the peregrines as they drop from the edge of their building before giving themselves over to air.

Now, I check that the Elegant Backstroker is not in my path as she completes her third lap, then duck my head under and swim towards the spot on the net where the seahorses make their home. Liz, a retired zoologist, told me she once saw a male in a tank change its colour to match that of a newly arrived female. They danced, too, just as Ranger John said. I didn't tell Liz that I also knew what it was to dance and be changed as a result.

When the male seahorse died, Zoologist Liz said, the female only survived him by twenty-four hours. I assumed she expired from grief, but Liz snorted and said, *It was probably the same virus that had taken the male, you sentimental git. Creatures don't fret and angst. They get on with living.*

After Peter died, the funeral director warned me there was an increased risk of heart attack for months after the death of a life partner. Back then, I wasn't convinced I wanted my heart to keep beating. I saw no point. But even if I had, what could I have done to stop the winged thing from swooping?

'You okay?' my sister Alanna asked as we walked home in grey cold air.

'Why are they parlours?'

She sped up to keep pace with me. 'What?'

'Why do funeral directors have parlours and not shopfronts or counters?'

'So . . . not okay then?'

'What about that coffin for forty thousand dollars? The Promethean. Do these people even know who Prometheus was? That his liver got eaten by an eagle, plucked out of his body, every day on repeat? Lead lining, for fuck's sake. You'd think a funeral director would know better than to dish up such shit.'

'Yep. Utter tripe,' Alanna said, and we both grimaced. One word was all it took to recall years of revulsion at our grandmother's favourite food. Some memories stick like glue.

Up ahead, Marina is backstroking. Soon, we will have to leave. She has a day at the easel, and I have to return to my desk, where some darlings must be killed like pigeons ended by peregrines. I've kept those words too long. They're death sentences, no matter how attached I've become to them.

How does a falcon put aside fellow feeling for another feathered creature, to kill it? How did my father slit the throat of a sheep? Or my grandmother chop the heads from her prized chooks?

Zoologist Liz strolls the shore, collecting sea glass. Chunks of milky greens and blues wash up after storms, enticing foragers and collectors. The ocean takes shattered shards and tumbles them about, softening their edges over weeks and months, just as my family and friends did for me after Peter died. The glass undergoes *a sea change into something rich and strange*, as Ariel sings in *The Tempest*.

I have two pieces of sea glass, collected on a high winter tide, in a jar on my coffee table. They catch the light, winking at me in the late afternoon sunshine. With them is a white shell I picked up on a beach in northern Spain, at the end of my 1300-kilometre pilgrimage. Its ribs are chalky and thick, like picked-over bones. There's a fragment of blue-and-white tile in that jar, too: salvaged on a woodland path in southern France, where I walked in Peter's memory. The dense green light of the forest made me claustrophobic, and I held the broken tile until I emerged into sunshine. It's a talisman . . .

. . . an object marked with magic signs and believed to confer on its bearer supernatural powers or protection . . .

It was just rubbish, dumped by someone renovating a kitchen, but it was the colour of the cornflowers we'd grown in our back courtyard, and the ceramic was cool in my hot, fearful hand. It seemed put there to comfort me.

These objects form a still life, one of several in my flat. I arrange and rearrange them, creating visual stories to anchor myself to here and now, then and there.

The Old Salt waves from the shore as I head for the net. It seems normal to him that I'm a swimmer, but Peter would be gobsmacked. Once, at a beach on the Southern Ocean, we threw off our clothes and raced into the water. I clung to his shoulders like a limpet, and, before I could process what was happening, we were out beyond the waves. With a hand under my back, he coaxed me to float. I lay there, willing my breath to settle, trying to yield, but my heartbeat was louder than his voice, so I latched onto his shoulders and he swam us in. On the sand, both of us gasped for air, like fish stranded out of water, never more alive than in the fear that death might be near.

In our early days, Peter would hyperventilate. The first time it happened we were at dinner in a fancy restaurant by the water—it may have been our first meal together—and he left the table abruptly. We'd been tentatively sharing our plausible and implausible dreams, when he let go of my hand, pushed back his chair and left. I didn't know him; didn't know what this behaviour meant; didn't know if I'd given pain. I watched the door. The candle dripped wax onto the tablecloth. The waiter topped up my glass and folded Peter's napkin.

Eventually, I decided to look for him. He was near the sea wall, leaning forward, hands on knees, sucking in salty air.

I approached tentatively. 'Are you okay?'

Ridiculous trio of words, trying to do so much work in nervous shorthand.

He straightened. Yes, he said, yes he was, but it was just that sometimes, when we were together, breath left him. It was like he couldn't take in air because he was overfull with emotion.

At the time I was flattered. Clearly this meant his feelings for me were unprecedented, presumably awesome. Later, though, I wondered whether it was because all feelings were potentially daunting. The polite world in which he'd grown up was so different from the messiness of mine. Feeling was what I knew best, even when I got it wrong. He was more comfortable when thinking—or acting, of course. There, he could sing and rage and take up space, breathing freely in other identities.

When he died, my identity changed.

widow

1. *A woman who has lost her husband by death and has not married again*

A line of print appearing alone at the top of a page can be interpreted as being unsightly, and is referred to by typesetters as a *widow*.

The *black widow* is a predator with a deadly bite, and yet widowhood is a passive state. You can't widow yourself. You must *be* widowed.

Architecture has *widow's walks*—rooftop platforms on coastal homes where the wives of mariners could pace, waiting for the sea to return their husbands.

Lusty widow . . . young widow . . . dangerous . . .

These were terms I'd heard daily when I directed a production of John Webster's play *The Duchess of Malfi*. A widow, one actor observed, is someone who has survived a brutal blow. Consequences are insignificant to her because she herself is no longer of any worth.

After Peter's death, I felt I'd become a shadow thing that should live a crone's life in a cave or fling herself onto a pyre; a spectre sucking the light and making others speak in hushed voices. After all, I had 'lost' my husband. I'd treated him like a pair of cheap sunglasses, or a telephone charger left in a hotel room. I vowed never to 'lose' anyone again. I would be permanently vigilant.

———

The water is opaque out here; murkier. I picture wraiths and phantoms, the drowned and shipwrecked dancing with the black stingray that sometimes slips under the net. Silky shadows and ghosts with pearls for eyes waft just out of sight. In *The Tempest,* Ariel's sea is *never-surfeited.* Something flutters in my chest. My breathing gets shallower as I go deeper.

Roll and breathe . . . slow and breathe . . .

One day, inspecting shells on the rocks, Zoologist Liz explained that a limpet is a kind of aquatic snail. I showed her the tattoo inside the fourth finger of my right hand.

'Why a snail?'

'It's a reminder,' I said. 'To slow down.'

She laughed. 'Good luck with that.'

My father has had to master snail's pace. 'You play the cards you're dealt, sweetheart.'

Over on the west coast of the continent, not far from the impossible aqua of the Indian Ocean and the beach where I first heard its unexpected roar—no one had warned me the sea was noisy—Dad will be snoozing. He used to rise before the magpies to begin his working day. Even when he retired, he would still go at sunrise to Fremantle's pristine Port Beach, stepping along its three-kilometre stretch of snowy sand.

Now, he sleeps late if he can. It's a relief when he doesn't wake in the night, breath catching and lungs filling with fluid.

Sometimes, he says, oxygen comes in easy ribbons. Some mornings, the panic of drowning in mid-air is forgotten. Then, he says, a cigarette never tastes so good. When we dare to suggest that smoking exacerbates emphysema, he flares: 'It's not emphysema! I've just got a bit of trouble breathing.'

He makes lemonade from the fruit of the neighbour's tree. A batch might take all morning. He squeezes, stops, strains, rests, squeezes, rests. He offered me a glass when I visited last summer, before the borders shut, and I savoured the bittersweet liquid.

'Did you enjoy that?' Dad asked. 'You sure took your time.'

Marina has slowed just enough for me to tuck in behind, patter-kicking in her wake. I follow her shimmer-trail out to where the seahorses wriggle. My fingers loosen and, as I stroke, water courses between them. They are mine and they are my mother's, familial fronds carrying me forward, through her atoms, through Peter's . . .

The possibility of an ending is always there, but for this moment, with bubbles leading the way, there is happiness. I kick with my toes, which are my father's, and I've almost caught up with Marina. She takes for granted that I can go where she leads, but I am still discovering the creature I'm becoming. Who is this swimmer? I think, as my right hand creates a billow of bubbles below me. Who is this woman, gliding with the tide?

IT'S COLD UNDER the shower, yet I linger, icy water needling my flesh. Feel it, I tell myself. Relish it. You're here, you're breathing, so wriggle.

ecstasy
1. *an overwhelming feeling of joy or rapture*

No, that's not it. It's not joy or rapture, although there is definitely pleasure, which is why I remain, despite the potential brain freeze.

And it occurs to me. It's discovery. I'm remaking myself. My tectonic plates are shifting.

(If I do remake myself, am I deserting you, Pete?)

A blast of chill wind from the south takes away all my breath, so I towel hard, making blood rush to the surface.

This morning I will put words on a page. I will stay the course. Then, I will head out, dressed in my funereal best. Afterwards, I will speak to Dad and cook a pot of lentils, and in the late afternoon I will walk. So, let the wind sting and the sand prickle. Why shouldn't there be a price for all this living?

I wrap myself in my robe, slip out of my swimmers, then pull up my hood as a thought creeps in, unbidden.

I wish he had not taken *eustasy* to bed that night. I wish he'd underlined *ecstasy* instead. That's a word to invite between the covers; a word to roll around on white linen. Not winding sheets—no, not morgues or coroners—but sheets that rustle like lazy splashes onto a shore. If he had chosen *ecstasy*, maybe . . .

A kookaburra laughs from the branch overhead. When I look up, he stops, shakes his head, and flies away. He has no time for fools or *ifs* or *maybes*; not while there are worms to be had.

THIS VIRUS HAS no respect for ritual. Even at a funeral, we're distanced, straining to recognise familiars, reluctant to embrace. It's an unseasonably hot day, and we're here, sweating behind our masks, to farewell an ebullient bloke who died after years of living with dementia. It was as though the seahorses in his brain had relocated.

His wife tended to him all through those times. She's a regular swimmer at Shark Beach, holding on to the net to ease in and out of the water. She was already well acquainted with loss, but now she is a widow, and she's rattled by this new persona. 'You'll have to teach me how to do it,' she said when I called on her. 'You know all about it.'

I know nothing. Who does? But she will be held. The eulogies from her tribe of adult children are full of chiacking and tenderness. We mourners laugh loud and cry buckets under the nave of the sandstone church, so I don't hear my phone's muted buzzing. It's only afterwards, in the glare on the church steps, when the same word is being said over and over like a mantra, that I understand our days are about to change.

Lockdown.

Lockdown.

Lockdown.

From midnight tonight, they say. Just this corner of the city, where Covid has a stronghold, they say. The premier resisted shutting down for too long, they say. It's Delta. It's a dark thing from the deep. It's an invisible thing in the air. It's about to swoop.

Those who had dropped their guard pull masks back over noses. They scurry to shop for groceries before attending the wake. The supermarket already has a queue out front, even though we've been told we can leave home any time to shop for food.

I hurry to my car and drive to the art gallery, fielding calls all the way. The first to phone are my sisters in Melbourne, Alanna and Amanda. Yes, another Amanda—the name means loveable, and in my experience of my little sister and my friends who bear the name it's totally accurate. Like all Melburnians, my sisters are veterans of months of curfews, homeschooling, Zoom meetings, online cooking schools and virtual book groups. They empathise, though I hear their apprehension that they will soon follow. I try to reassure them—our health officials have said it will only be for a week; they will contain the spread as they've done before; it won't cross the border—but my words sound lame.

I park above the Botanic Gardens and walk, in bright sunshine, chatting to my brothers. They're sympathetic, but because they live in Western Australia, they can't fully understand. Remoteness, along with that relentlessly closed border, means they've not experienced the daily dilemma of second-guessing whether it's safe to turn up to a workplace or a doctor's surgery, a supermarket or hardware shop. I'm glad for them, and for the security for Dad, even as I resent being kept out.

I stop in the shade of a Moreton Bay fig to call him. We chat about the Sudoku puzzle and the nine-letter word in his morning newspaper. He likes to finish both before going out to greet his magpies and ravens. Not crows: 'We have ravens over here, sweetheart.'

'What's in a name, Dad?'

'That's rich, coming from my pedant daughter!'

The lockdown hasn't registered with him yet, though he does comment that he never thought he would see the day when we'd be kept from our families by law. He has managed to find some breath, he tells me, and thinks he will water the roses. This is often code for going outside to have a smoke, but today I'm not sure. He says he has gone back to bed 'for a rest', though it's only mid-morning there.

Dad has seven rosebushes growing in a narrow strip of sand along the back of his unit. His favourite produces a deep red flower, and its perfume is unusually fruity. There's a bud on it, he says, coughing—he can see it from his window—so he wants to give it a nudge. He'll get to it. It's a good day with no clouds anywhere. He's on song, he insists.

I enter the gallery. Under its soaring ceilings and along the cool marble halls the world feels calm and ordered. I wander without a destination—yes, Pete, I'm flâneuring—from the Indigenous galleries to the Europeans, from the contemporary to the traditional. Eventually, inevitably, I stop in front of my favourite work. It's a small still life: a scarlet waratah in a dimpled turquoise vase in front of a background of geometric shapes that look, to my untrained eye, like they're influenced by traditional Islamic art, or maybe even tiling. It was painted in 1887 by a Frenchman called Lucien Henry, but it could have been created last week by Marina, who also uses patterns in her work.

I didn't understand the impulse to come here when lockdown was announced, but standing in front of Henry's work, I settle. It's a familiar. If I can't see family, I will see it. It's an antidote to my dread of funerals and the mayhem of lockdown. It survived the Spanish flu and it will be here after this pandemic. There will still be life in its crimson petals; its Indian Ocean blue will not fade.

I have a handsome book of Lucien Henry's work; a catalogue from an exhibition I didn't see. I often flick through the pages, admiring the originality of his vision of his adopted country and its natural wonders, wishing I could have seen his lyrebird chair and waratah candelabra.

A retrospective is not possible for writers or musicians in the way it is for a visual artist, where a viewer can stand in a room and, in a turn of the head, sweep across decades, seeing connections and influences, understanding the ebbs and flows of a life's curiosities and fascinations. For the artist, there must be both gratification and astonishment in having all those memories throbbing from the walls; in recalling where works were made and who was with them as brush dipped into paint. A lifetime, right there.

I take one last internal snapshot of my waratah. As I head for home, I notice the spiky crimson heads of Gymea lilies against a cerulean sky. Once again, Lucien has shown me how to see.

This lockdown means I surely won't get to Perth for Dad's ninety-first. They say compassionate visits are allowed, but last time I applied, when he was taken to hospital with lungs full of fluid, I was advised to *call back if your father goes into intensive care.* They're expert at keeping intruders out, over there. For fifty years, they've had a program to stop starlings from crossing the border. The feathered intruders are trapped the minute they're spied.

After washing and drying my bowl and spoon from breakfast, I head for the computer. There's no news, but that doesn't stop me staring into the screen, trying to fathom the day's headlines. Here's another new word, Pete: *doom-scrolling*. I'm searching without looking; following a cursor but not comprehending. I remember something like this from the days after you died, that fuzzy non-thinking. Back then, tasks were the only things that helped. So . . .

I water the succulents on the balcony.

I strip the bed and remake it.

I take a load of washing down to the shared laundry.

I snip the wicks of candles.

I dust and rearrange photographs. There's Dad as a blond cherub in rompers.

In winter sunshine, I hang washing on the lines out the back.

I make tea, of course.

Eventually, I return to the news sites, but my stomach churns, so I click across to the peregrine falcon home page, hoping they might have arrived early to their Melbourne high-rise, but of course there's nothing. The webmaster invites bird lovers to tune in for the season when it begins in August. I have six weeks to wait, and yet I stay, as though the act of staring will console me.

I would stare like this when I was small, in Perth, waiting for Dad to arrive home from the factory, called Pegasus, where they made horseshoes. The name struck me as strange, having read a book about mythic creatures: why would a horse with wings need to bother with footwear? Pegasus was located in an industrial part of town, a world away from the bush where Dad had lived when he and Mum were together. When my brother and I came south on our holiday visits, it was a novelty to go to Dad's work with its fizzing sparks and metallic smells, but mostly Brett and I passed the days with our stepmother.

Brett didn't like the city and couldn't wait to get back to Mum and our stepfather on their farm, but I didn't mind it; there were kids next door and over the road, and we would write and perform plays in the garage—my first dip into theatrical waters. And there were libraries. My stepmother would take me to the local branch, and I'd come home with arms chock-full of books. I couldn't believe I was allowed so many, so often. I was accustomed to waiting for a parcel on a truck or, later, to re-reading the entire collection of our two-teacher school.

In the city, I'd lose myself among the library shelves, then again for long silent hours when we got home, intrigued by underlines and turned-down corners, trying to decipher what was important to others and why. (I'm seeing a pattern here, Pete.)

But nearing sunset, I could be found seated on the stone letterbox, crushing the spongy flower heads of a handy lavender plant between my fingers, staring at the bend in our road, willing Dad to come home from the place of the horse with wings. I stared hard, in just the way the falcon chicks stare at the sky as they wait for food, or as I've seen Dad stare out the kitchen window into the car park of his units, observing the comings and goings, in case one of them is for him. Staring, as though there were power in a gaze.

Down in Melbourne, on that first icy widowed morning, I'd stared into Peter's still life the same way. The dictionary. The French book. The apple and mug. I was waiting for the thumping sound of the engine of his old car, even though it was parked out the back; waiting for him to arrive with irises and party pies, distracted and whistling.

I'd spoken of practicalities with his sister and her husband and taken phone calls from the coroner and police, but it was the collection of familiar objects that held me. Our ordinary life lay there on our coffee table, insisting on a dailiness that might yet make a lie of the new normal I was being asked to accept. Surely, if I paid enough attention, if I stared long enough, I could remake the world.

After all, there was no body. I had only other people's words to explain his absence. The objects were tangible: his fingers on the pages, his lips on the mug. I inspected that still life from every angle, imprinting it, interrogating it, looking into the guts of it—just as I'm doing now, back at the computer screen, staring again, searching for how to be or what to do. The only reply that comes, and keeps coming on every website, is that single word.

Lockdown.

Your dictionary has no definition for this new version of the word, Pete. There is so much it doesn't know, now. We have *super-spreader* events. We have *waist-up dressing* for *Zoom*—which does not mean *to move rapidly*, as you might expect. We have the *quarantini*—a drink you have at the end of a day of *iso*. There is the *Coronacut*—I gave myself one with nail scissors, and it wasn't bad. There are *Covidiots* who don't wash their hands with *sanny*. We have *flattened curves* and *self-isolation*. Language is changing with us, leaving you further and further behind.

How would you have coped with lockdowns? You'd have read, I imagine; researched plagues and solitude. You'd have sought out Camus; returned to *Year of Wonders* . . .

Books. I will need books.

I grab a mask and dash down to the one-room library opposite the harbour baths. I sign in, sanitise, then cruise the shelves, grabbing at novels, philosophy and memoir. The older of the two librarians says I'm never again allowed to scoff at those who panic buy toilet paper.

The walk uphill is slowed by the weight of other people's words. I stop under a frangipani to look towards the city skyline. Across the water, workers are going about their day, not cancelling appointments or shopping for extra masks but shooing hungry ibises from rubbish bins or planning after-work drinks. As I climb the stairs, I make a mental note to tell my voice agent I'd be happy to go into a studio if work should arise.

Happy? I'd be on my knees in gratitude.

I flick the switch on the kettle. The clock that was a wedding present ticks as the water rumbles. Only a week, that's what they say.

The afternoon holds its breath. Lockdown minus eight hours.

A cockatoo lands on the tip of the neighbour's pine tree, stretching its wings and its butter-yellow mohawk. A lone cloud drifts from right to left across the empty sky—and my hippocampi play a trick. They retrieve a memory from way down in my personal deep, delivering me from my kitchen in steamy Sydney to the arid bush of my early childhood. The sky there is also uninterrupted blue, but the light is harsher, and the dust is orange between my bare toes. I don't hear the water boil or the switch flick off, as I observe my lanky young dad skinning the kangaroo he has strung to a beam.

This was not unusual. Dad had to feed us: his family, the jackaroos and the working dogs. Usually it was a sheep, but sometimes it was a roo. Feeling no squeamishness, I focus intently on each swipe of the blade, waiting for the creature's guts to spill onto the ground, so I can peer deep into them and read their secrets.

Later in the day, my grandmother, known as Ning, will make an aromatic soup from the kangaroo's tail. She might also chop off the head of a chook, as she does for special occasions, like birthday dinners. I will watch this too, and after the bird has finished running headless circuits, I will sit with Ning while she plucks its speckled feathers.

I'd learned from observation that kangaroos had two stomachs and chewed their food to get every bit of goodness from it, in just the way that Mum would tell me to eat my dinner—and in just the way that, now, Dad must chew and chew his food, because he can no longer produce saliva. Swallowing has become a conscious task, and he must take a sip of water—or preferably wine!—with every bite.

I sip tea and consider the memory, examining it for flaws. It came unbidden, and it's not from a story I've been told. It both unsettles and thrills. There was no photo of those images, no recording of the sounds. Those reclaimed moments are mine, and I want to stay with them, but phone calls and text messages, 'alerts' and emails, bleat.

When Mum died, the world hushed. It was in the days before mobile phones and internet, long before text messages could find us everywhere. Alanna and I sat, red-eyed and disbelieving, after she stopped breathing. Staff tiptoed and whispered. There were no announcements or 'posts'. Only silence.

If anything confirmed that Mum was gone, it was that. In life, wherever she was, there had been noise and hustle, silliness and clamour. It's my recurring memory of her.

'Come on, we're late. Get in the car, small fry.'

And yes, she did call us her 'fry'. I never knew the word

referred to the offspring of sea creatures. Like so much she said and did, it was just taken for granted as we tried to keep up.

'I don't give a damn who has the front seat, just hop in. We're late. Hurry *up*.'

We were always late, always jumbled; always packing a bag and racing to keep up as Mum found a bigger place for less rent, or somewhere that reminded her of the bush; always transferring from car to car, from mother to father, house to house.

I get confused when people ask me where I grew up. There was no family home. I can only tell them who cared for me. Home was an oversized cast of parents and step-parents, friends and lovers. Mum married three times. Dad married twice. Both had other partners. Their five adult 'fry' are now spread across the continent, in three cities and one country town. But when Mum died, it was like the aftermath of a storm. Everything and everyone was muted.

Now, just as when news of Peter's death was posted on Facebook before I could tell some of those who loved him most, the world bristles with connection. Neighbours express relief that a decision has been made.

'We'll need to wear masks in the stairwells, of course.'

This outbreak began at a cafe just up the hill—a friend had been there on the very morning, she emails—and it spread like the grassfires I'd seen as a kid, when Mum would make sandwiches and gallons of tea for the men who were back-burning.

As the sun starts to dive, the sky flares. I phone a friend who lives down the hill. He has just turned eighty-seven and has been having intensive radiotherapy for the last six months, so I imagine he will be exhausted, but when I tell him I'm going for a sunset stroll, he asks if I'd like company. I shouldn't be surprised. He's the original *peregrino*, having completed several *caminos* in his time. He likes to tell the story of how he marked his seventy-fifth birthday by walking 500 kilometres in open-toed sandals. Still, his cancer treatment is sapping energy and strength, so it will be a gentle saunter. We meet on the corner and set off, taking the harbour path, a couple of pilgrims winding down the day.

On the pavement beside the dinghies, social distancing is observed in a jokey, hail-fellow-well-met display of good cheer, but the vibe is nervous and hyper. We're all Covid-weary after fifteen months of living with the virus, but also excited by this change of gear. We have no idea how much wearier we'll become.

The Pilgrim and I veer—slowly, slowly—up to the cliffs, in time to catch a strawberry moon rising from the Pacific, burnishing a path across the ocean. It's easy to imagine it's solid, the ripples like golden steps. I could drop down to follow that watery road out to the horizon—but of course it would only take me further east.

I turn to the west, to the bronzing skyscrapers. The Pilgrim inquires after Dad; they met a few years earlier, when my father flew east to see where I had made my home. It was only his second trip to Sydney. He couldn't take his eyes off the Opera House as we passed it on a ferry, twisting and leaning to view it from every angle. It hadn't been built when he first visited. He's weary, I tell the Pilgrim, who nods, hunching his shoulders against the wind.

I click photos, then we walk home via the overgrown tram track, which is my preferred route because tourists never take it. By the end of lockdown, the council will have transformed it into a manicured diversion through the remnant rainforest, and my resentment will have turned to admiration. But I don't know that yet, and mumble that I wish the lockdown might halt their plans.

You can't stop progress, my friend says as we part ways, and I watch him head for home, his pace steady.

Further west, the sun will be almost over the yardarm, and if it has been a good day, Dad will be pouring a wine. I call him as I make for home, chatting to him through my face mask. He has breath today, he tells me—and a cigarette in his hand. I don't want him to hear my irritation, so I tell him about the memory of the kangaroo and the guts.

'No, darling, that wasn't me,' he says.

'But I'm sure,' I say. 'It's not from a photo. No one told me.'

'Mm.' He coughs, clears his throat. 'Maybe it was one of the jackaroos. Or maybe it happened when Mum had the farm.' He pauses, but I don't speak. 'I'm not saying you didn't see it, honey, but it wasn't me. I wouldn't have killed with you around.'

I listen as he inhales more poison. I'd been so sure.

'Oh,' is all I manage to say.

I upload photos to Instagram, then make dinner while chatting to Alanna in Melbourne. I light candles and settle on the couch to watch the news, unaware that this will become a daily ritual: walk by the water at sunset, post an image, talk to Dad, prepare food in remote company and eat in solitude while watching a cascade of increasingly grim headlines. I have no notion of how long it will be before another human will enter my home, or how I will come to depend on things with feathers.

Still life with
papers

SICKLY SUNLIGHT CAUGHT the edge of a sheaf of typewritten pages lying on sand-coloured carpet. On top of them sat a bulky paperback, its white cover embossed with leaves and flowers; and beside it, a notebook. That was illustrated with a line-drawing of the Eiffel Tower rising from a jumble of grey apartment buildings, and, in flowing script, a quotation: *Paris is always a good idea—Audrey Hepburn*. Tucked inside the notebook were several pages of thick cream paper, covered with navy-blue cursive scrawl.

Lying alone, to the right of that main grouping, was an envelope, one side torn open. Creases revealed where it had been folded, perhaps to fit inside a pocket. Written on it was a dot-point list.

———

The last seconds of Peter's life were right there, on the carpet beside our bed, easy to read and easy enough to understand. The only surprise was the book: *On Extinction*. I'd given it to him three Christmases earlier, and underneath my inscription was his rating. It had earned two ticks.

Our Christmas days were quiet. We'd celebrate with breakfast, which was my mother's tradition. It began from necessity when, as children, Brett and I would go to Dad for Christmas lunch, but I kept it up when I left home. The menu was hers too—scrambled eggs, toast, and a dish of onions, tomatoes, basil and black pepper, cooked until it's almost the consistency of chutney. Tea, of course. Multiple cups. Then, when breakfast was done, gifts. Peter and I always gave each other a book.

When do behaviours become rituals? When does something evolve into a personal tradition, something you can't imagine dishonouring? Christmas without a book was unthinkable—from our very first year, when I gave him a copy of 'The Owl and the Pussy-cat', an illustrated *Kama Sutra* and Shirley Hazzard's *The Transit of Venus*.

The rest of our day would be spent reading in festive silence. We'd break for snacks and more tea, or stroll the neighbourhood to see which kids had received which toys. Some years, if the weather was mild, we'd drive up to the shack, where we'd wander to the river to read under a gnarled apple tree until the sun moved too far west. Then we'd return to the verandah, put our feet up on the rickety wooden rail, and continue reading. That was Christmas.

Now, with the help of an inspired bookseller, I keep the tradition alive. Late in December, Elizabeth will call to say she has a parcel waiting. She will have considered new releases and classics, translations and picture books, to find something I won't anticipate. Sometimes she puts annotations into the text, or post-it notes with commentary, to create the kind of dialogue I might once have had with Peter. She was nervous the first year I asked her to choose.

'What if I pick the wrong book?'

Peter and I chose plenty of wrong 'uns, I told her—but *On Extinction* had been a success.

That said, I hadn't known he was re-reading it. Perhaps it was connected to *eustasy* and the changes in sea level. Maybe, after discovering the word in his dictionary, he'd left his tea and apple core to go down the back to his studio to locate the book. He'd have stood in the icy air, distracted, as he searched for the relevant chapter. Then he'd have shivered and scarpered back into the house and up the hallway, leafing through pages. He'd have snuggled under the covers to warm his ever-cold toes and begin prep for the morning's shoot. He did some of his best work in bed.

The day after he died, he was to have begun filming for the new TV series. I can't remember its name, but I do recall the producers sent me a cube-shaped box of perfect white rosebuds in memory of him. But that was later. If the tectonic plates hadn't shifted, he would have been on set, rehearsing a scene or joking with fellow actors at the very moment I was staring at that book on our bedroom floor, trying not to see the pink stains on his pillow or hear the sinister silence of a place that had once been all quotidian safety.

We'd discussed that word—*quotidian*—only a few days before.

adj. 1. daily, of every day
    2. commonplace, trivial
n. (in full quotidian fever) a fever recurring every day

When Peter died, I was recovering from glandular fever, but he was rock-steady, as quotidian as the bedside still life, which was like countless others I'd seen when I drew back the curtains to let in the morning sun.

There was the script for his television scenes, with his lines marked in optimistic blue. We'd read them onto his mini-recorder before I left for Sydney. Line-learning and testing were ordinary activities, commonplace, like the days before I'd left, when we'd strolled under street trees—ornamental pears turning gold—to the cinema. We'd eaten takeaway Thai for a treat. I'd made minestrone and stewed rhubarb to stock the fridge. Red foods, both. Did that explain the stains?

The cream pages were a letter from me. The night before I flew to Sydney, we had lain in bed, heads almost touching, discussing whether we could move, for a time, to France. Ever

since high school, when he'd befriended a French exchange
student and won a language prize, he had dreamed he might
live there. He'd been studying at the Alliance Française in the
years before his death and got to know a guy who bought and
renovated abandoned French houses, so the dream was not
beyond reach, although we'd have had to sell up to do it. I was
excited for him, and rose early to write, telling him so. I'd left
the letter in his car when he dropped me at the airport.

Writing to him was also commonplace. I did it when I was
away walking or working, when he was on tour with a play or
on a film shoot, and when I was up in my study and he was
downstairs making tea. I did it on post-it notes and embossed
paper, on recycled drafts of work and on postcard after postcard. Correspondence was a way of conversing at equal pace.
A letter could make order of my overexcited speech patterns
and feelings, and he could process them in his own time. So,
this letter beside the bed, though it was about new possibilities,
was definitely *quotidian*.

After his death, I found all my mail to him. He'd kept
every note, it seemed. Piles of letters tied with string, cards for
occasions or 'just because', handmade missives, brief notes and
epic tracts. So many words. They still sit in a storage box. I can't
part with them, but neither can I bring myself to re-read them.

Along with the letter, I'd given him the Paris notebook,
which I'd bought a few days earlier, before he'd raised the idea
of moving to France.

Always a good idea . . .

It wasn't prescience or premonition; just a wish to delight. He hadn't written in its pages, but he'd brought it in from the car and kept it close.

And then there was the list: the most quotidian of all. Covered with his cramped leftie's handwriting, it resembled so many others he'd made over the years, always on recycled envelopes. They were his way of organising everything from personal shortcomings to grocery items; from mistakes made to exercise goals to monies owing; from fantasy destinations to books read; from people he wanted to visit to climate and refugee actions; from jokes to regrets to Christmas cards; from trees planted to opportunities lost to songs to learn and weeds to pull. In the coming months, I'd find dozens of lists, some from long before we met.

This one, the one he had shown me that Sunday night before I flew to Sydney, lay, looking innocuous enough, waiting to become one of my most treasured possessions. It was the inventory of jobs that needed doing if we were to put our house on the market. He was going to ask his friend Chris, an actor and carpenter, to quote for the work.

Chris—12/5/14—Worth it? Sell/rent?
- Back studio window
- Doorhandles and locks
- Hallway floor creak
- Re-block corner

- Front room wall crack
- Verandah corner raise
- Side gate rebuild
- Fence post finial
- Bathroom creak/laundry cupboards
- 2 roof ladders?

And it continued . . .

I'd read it over his bare shoulder as he chatted away, suggesting we relocate to Sydney initially—*You've always wanted to return for longer than a visit*—while he investigated things French. An old friend of his had expressed interest in France too, he told me; she was also eager for upheaval. I was racing to keep up. I didn't know the Peter of this list—or if I did, I'd forgotten him.

When we met, in October 1986, I was a Sydney resident, having moved from Western Australia four years earlier. I loved my chosen city for its hilly topography and fecundity, which was startling to someone raised in the western flatlands.

In Sydney, water oozed from the sandstone behind gargantuan fig trees which dropped their squishy fruit onto sidewalks; heady-scented orange jessamine lined paths; mould sprouted inside unworn shoes and on the collars of jackets; frangipani flowers lolled on thick grass like fallen stars; the bark of the twisting angophora trees that ringed the harbour changed from cream to burnt red before being wantonly tossed off at season's end; mosses and lichens, combined with late afternoon downpours, made strolling a slippery activity. The city seemed restless and absurdly fertile, changing and growing ceaselessly.

I grew and changed too. With no history there, I was able to try new versions of myself, experimenting with who I might become. It was my first taste of the liberation of being a blank canvas, and although I often felt like an unsophisticated hick, still the city sang of reinvention and possibility. Sydney's neon nightlife, winding one-way mazes and crazy spires—religious and commercial side by side—were as enthralling as her foliage. I planned to stay for life.

Peter was from Melbourne. We met when I was down there performing in a play and he came backstage after the show to visit friends. My brain's seahorses danced up a storm, conjuring my first sighting of him, back in Perth, ten years earlier. He was on tour with a play, and I was a schoolgirl in a forest-green uniform, hungry to be one of the cast. My family had no experience of theatre, but in high school, drama and literature classes lit my days. Writers and actors were demi-gods, and I thought Peter was tremendous, able to convey a complicated internal life while rolling a cigarette or just leaning in a doorframe.

Backstage in the Melbourne dressing room, recalling him in that role made me shy. I'm sure we spoke, though I can't remember a word, but a month later there was a second take when we acted together for a fortnight in a radio drama.

We were playing circumstance-crossed lovers in an Australian period romance called *Policy and Passion*. In a memorable scene,

I had to suck snake venom from his arm. Trying to maintain dignity while standing at a microphone making slurping sounds onto my forearm, with him opposite acting monosyllabic stoicism, may have been the greatest test I ever encountered as an actor. The technicians gave us the out-takes as a wedding gift—ten minutes of helpless, uncontrollable corpsing.

In the theatre, that term is used when an actor is unable to maintain a straight face. It's worst—and funniest—at moments of intense emotion or tragedy. Suddenly, something—a word, the facial expression of a colleague or even just being in front of an audience—strikes you as absurd, and it becomes impossible not to laugh. It's terrifying and delicious. Like the giggles that can overwhelm mourners at a funeral, perhaps it's a form of catharsis, but I've never known why it's called *corpsing*. I checked Peter's reference dictionary, to no avail.

The theatre is loaded with superstitions and death imagery. Mention *Macbeth* (Peter once played the title role) in a dressing room and disaster will befall you. Quick! Go outside and turn around three times while whistling. When an actor comes offstage triumphant, they might say they *killed it*; when they feel they've failed, they'll say they *died out there*. In Elizabethan times, the roof over a stage was *the heavens*. Even now, the furthest seats are *the gods*, and a *ghost light* is left to burn when a theatre is empty.

On the final day of recording for our bodice-ripper, we'd rehearsed the 'garden proposal scene' several times but were worried it would sound stilted when we recorded it. During the lunch break, Peter bought freesias to scatter around the microphone, summoning the perfume of spring. We nailed the scene and adjourned for drinks in the legal district where, in a pub surrounded by silks and egos, I asked him to dance. Despite there being no music playing, he said yes, and just like seahorses changing colour, we were altered.

So began a crazy-fast courtship, to use a word from the radio play. We both fell. Hard and fast. We spent three all-consuming weeks together before he left on an extended study trip to New York. He'd arranged it before we met, and the ticket couldn't be changed, so we had to separate. This was high drama.

An answering machine was as modern as telephone technology got in those days, but because international calling rates were exorbitant, Peter wouldn't be leaving messages on mine. A separation would be exactly what the word said, so I bought us matching cloth-covered journals, and we pledged to write in them daily and exchange them on his return.

I've only ever kept a journal when I have a hunch something is going to be memorable: on long pilgrimage walks, a few overseas trips and for several volumes of outpourings in the year after Peter died—the Year of Firsts, as a friend called it, when she sent me an exquisite bound book to fill. I catalogued the days—first time I drove the car, first wedding anniversary, first Christmas without him—thinking I was recording my victory over the worst that could happen, and trying to exhaust myself so I'd sleep. Sometimes it took hours, scratching into the soft paper as cold crept in around windows and under doors. If I had no more to write but was still wired on grief's adrenaline, I would open his dictionary, hoping to locate meaning: a squiggle, a slash, a bracket. It was a conversation with him. Then I'd note what 'he' had said.

Now, I wish I'd recorded our quotidian days because my memory is so unreliable. Maybe it worsened after the shock of his death. Certainly, he was my memory bank for much of our shared life, and great chunks of my story burned with him.

I had no idea as I wrote through that first year that the second would be even worse, but part of me clearly did understand, back when I met Peter, that I was at the beginning of something momentous, and those journals are time capsules of the people we were then; still lifes in written form.

Reading Peter's in the days after he returned from New York (unannounced and four weeks early, on Christmas Eve) I encountered an impulsive dreamer; someone who acted on instincts and hunches. This was borne out by him proposing to me on Boxing Day. I put it down to jetlag, but the man in the journal had made flesh-and-blood Peter even more alluring, so I answered with a resounding *yes*. A month later, we drove down the highway to Melbourne in my yellow sedan. I took only what could be crammed into its compact interior and never missed a thing I'd left behind.

Maybe this was the precedent for all I discarded after he died; or maybe I learned it as a child, moving houses with Mum or between her place and Dad's. Maybe it's why I feel so at home when walking with only a backpack. Whatever, it could not have been more different from Peter, who was not impetuous, as I'd thought. In fact, he weighed possibilities, pondered options and researched rigorously before committing. Yes, he was a dreamer, but the person I'd fallen for was not quotidian Peter. There was no hint in our beginning of the man who wrestled daily with self-doubt and anxiety. I had to learn, and keep learning, the real person. Luckily, the essence of him—kindness, curiosity, whimsy and integrity—never wavered.

In fairness, I'm sure he'd tell you I was not entirely the person he'd met in the journal I kept for him. I was spinning in my own besotted orbit. I fell for the Peter who had fallen for me and vice versa.

I wonder if he would fall for this new person—the widow. She is overly vigilant about those she loves, panicking when they don't answer phones or text messages. Living alone has made her finicky, and she can't relax unless her bed is made just so. She is unable to leave the house unless her will is visible on the left-hand corner of her desk.

Could he tolerate a woman who tries to control life to such a degree? Would he stay with someone who'd monitor him constantly so he couldn't die suddenly? This widow is spikier and defensive without him to help her laugh at herself. She is uncertain where once she'd leap; weighing odds when once it was exciting to risk. If order is threatened, she becomes fractious, and she barks when asked about re-partnering. No, she does not want it. This widow can't imagine sharing her life again. She has no *widow's fire*.

(It's not in your dictionary, Pete, but people were quick to tell me about it—*an uncontrollable desire for sex following a bereavement*. I waited for it. Wondered if it might arrive to heat the winter nights. But there was no sign. I used to admire strangers' bodies, imagining textures and smells, fantasising about lips and skin. Was it your quotidian familiarity that made the unfamiliarity of others so alluring?)

His Paris notebook is still empty—it sits beside the cloth journals on the second shelf of my bookcase—and his list is beside me, in the top drawer of my desk. It's not something I would frame or show to others, but it's as meaningful as a wedding ring. It was written by the man of the first journals, not the man who battled self-doubt.

His dark days had always been a secret we guarded together. That grew more and more difficult over time, and finally I wrote to him—yes, another letter—saying I needed him to seek support from outside. And he'd done it. He found a counsellor who'd helped. It made me question whether I should have written that letter earlier. I liked being 'the sunshine in the house'. He used to call me that, but maybe I enabled his sadness.

Was I a partner in an unhealthy dance? I have no answers, even with hindsight's supposedly impeccable vision.

So, there we were on that Sunday night, in the bed in which he would die only a week later, talking about moving and changing, and he was speaking about feelings, too; and it was a confusing whirl, exciting and frightening, and this time it was me on the back foot. I was still glandular feverish. I said it was too fast; that we should consult someone about finances and France. I said we couldn't possibly sell both our home and the shack simultaneously. Ultimately, though, guided by his list on the envelope, that was exactly what I did.

THE FIRST MORNING of lockdown is much like any other. Walk. Swim. Work. Then, at 11 a.m., the premier and chief medical officer hold a press conference, announcing that from today the entire city will be locked down. Now we're all in this together, as the song goes ad nauseum. I turn off the television and return to my desk.

During our first lockdown, fifteen months ago, I vowed to make solitude count. I would use the time to finish the project that had caused me so much angst. I'd read classics, write proper letters, refresh my French and Italian grammar, listen to Spanish podcasts, study Peter's dictionary for half an hour every day. With my self-devised Corona Curriculum, I would kick Covid to the kerb.

Those best-laid plans went astray, of course. A crawling nausea lurked under my resolve and, eventually, I managed to identify it. Lockdown was exactly like the initial waves of post-Peter grief. Sleepless nights of fretfulness; an inability to focus or retain information because of anxiety's roar; purpose removed; and always the dread that someone, somewhere, would be taken and I wouldn't be there to rescue them. Once again, the abyss was close, a camouflaged pit we could not avoid.

Not this time, I tell myself. No. This time I will go with the tides. I will flow.

In my lunch break, I call Dad, but he is off song, so we cut it short. I'm not overly concerned, because Judy, his partner, is coming to visit him, and she will lift his spirits. Recently, Dad told me they were 'developing a lovely relationship', and I snorted my tea with laughter. They've been together for thirty years, despite (or maybe because of) never having lived in the same house. She's a fanatical golfer, and although he has never played, he's proud of her prowess, and of her devotion to her family. They've picnicked, danced and partied, but they've also done their share of hard yards. Dad adores Judy. Perhaps she's the reason he calls himself Lucky.

I try to work while fielding the pings of emails and texts, but in the late afternoon I shut up shop and call the Pilgrim. His energy is low, but yes, he would enjoy a stroll.

Down by the ferry wharf, masked locals mill about, gossiping and conjecturing, under a scavenge of seagulls. My camera captures the raucous birds, diving and protesting, against a backdrop of molten gold clouds. *I came over all Tippi Hedren,* someone writes on my Instagram post. The image contains the uneasiness of the day, transformed into roiling beauty.

Six hours later, blanketed by darkness and a knee rug, I settle on the balcony. The neighbours are playing a song I know by heart, its lyrics drifting up through the bamboo and palms, urging me to come closer, to dance . . .

Something rustles in the eucalypt. Up on the cliffs, a dog howls. The moon drifts, languid and heavy, just as it did over the bay in Melbourne when we stopped the car on our first night, because it was all happening too fast, after I'd asked Peter to dance with me in that pub with no music, and we did, we danced around and around and out the door, into his car, hurtling through the dark, the heater up high, until he stopped and turned off the motor and we stood in clear night air, breathing each other in as we gazed at a pathway made by the moon on the water—a loony moon, just like the one that's dancing over me and my neighbours.

Every night before bed, Peter the night owl would step outside to consult the sky. This 'looking up' was as important to him as any Oxford definition, and a report about the constellations would be brought to me before I fell asleep. I maintained his ritual, gazing through his binoculars as though they were his eyes, trying to read the stars like leaves in a celestial teapot, just as I'm doing now, in the company of flying foxes on serrated wings, and over there, beyond the pine tree, a hunting owl, calling *who, who, who* . . .

I get up to consult his dictionary. I want to know whether the fat glowing orb overhead is a harvest moon, like the one in the song. Surely, it's a sign.

But no. The entry on page 644 is unequivocal: a *harvest* moon occurs closest to the autumn equinox, and we are now a month into winter. Disappointed, I shift the magnifying glass over the column of words, landing on an entry three above: *haruspex*. It was the title given to a 'religious official' in ancient Rome who interpreted omens by inspecting animal's entrails. What would a *haruspex* divine from the intestines of a fish choked by cling wrap? Sacrifices would undoubtedly be required. And what might a *haruspex* make of my innards, were I to be split open like that kangaroo I'm so sure I remember?

The place where I spent my earliest years was inhabited tens of thousands of years before there was a Roman Empire, and those people were great storytellers. It was Lois who told me about the man with feathered feet. We were playing under a picture of two barefoot white children huddling together in a tempest, trying to cross a crumbling wooden bridge. A moon sailed behind dark clouds while a woman wearing a cascading gown, her fair hair flowing over enormous wings, hung in mid-air, keeping watch over the little ones.

Lois liked the picture. Pretty feathers, she said, but you wouldn't want to see them for real. A flying woman would be scary. But if ever I saw a man with feathers on his feet, she told me, I was done for.

That's my first recollection of the overlapping stories that formed me. As a child, I felt no tension between the tales of snakes and goannas I heard while digging in the creek bed and the serpent stories nuns told in school. I never questioned the myriad 'coincidences' in my days, either. It wasn't mind-reading or oogly-boogly magic; just people knowing things in different ways. My mother was even more steeped in contradictions and myths, and would tell us about our lives as though we were characters in an epic.

You were born at the bottom of the world, on the edge of a vast ocean. Before your eyes could focus, I took you to a place where you grew strong out of red earth . . .

My childhood memories are like the flickering images we'd see on the walls of the local hall, when travelling pictures came to town and were screened on two bedsheets. That was in Yalgoo—the second town in which I attended school. One pub. One general store. Just like the village where I live now, except here I'm surrounded by water and there it was burnt orange dust that stained Brett's snowy hair when he rode in the back of the ute. I remember none of the serials or movies we saw then, but I do recall having a terrible crush on our teachers, Mr and Mrs Byrnes. She had slender bowlegs and wore high heels in the dusty playground. He was more handsome than any celluloid hero.

I remember drifting with a schoolfriend in the icy water of our house tank towards the spongy green moss that coated the walls. We were in the sky, in the clouds, in our floaties. I hear the hiss of bubble and squeak in the frypan; see beady-eyed emus at the gate; feel sweet water-bag water spilling down my chest. But how do I know they're not just tales I was told? Can I trust my wayward seahorses?

I return to the balcony. Air hangs like a wet towel as the song repeats. A bat squeaks in the palm tree. With his wings wrapped around himself, he looks like an overripe fruit. I snuggle under my rug and stare at the stars, trying to read my own guts.

A friend sewed this blanket for me after Peter died. It's patchwork, with images of things I love stitched onto it: flowers, the countryside, broccoli and a picture of my little nephews. (One of them wrote me a card. *Don't worry*, he printed carefully. *You still have us.*) On the reverse is a night sky: stars and moons against black. Back then, I would sit in our living room with it covering my lap as I recited the Bardo prayer I'd been given by a Buddhist friend.

Peter has taken the great leap . . .

I took comfort from its implication that he'd done something bold, even if that meant he'd chosen to leave. It was better than thinking of him alone, unable to call for help.

My Buddhist friend asked about words he'd heard at the funeral. 'Why say *eternal life grant unto him*? Why would you want that?'

I didn't have an answer. I didn't ask why he thought it possible to come back as a dog or a butterfly, either. If ritual connects you to something safe, enact it. If a story is salve, tell it.

Buddhists say the Bardo prayer for forty-nine days after a death, because there is no way of knowing when a person might transition to their next life, but they believe it occurs within that period. On night thirty-five, I wondered why I was continuing with a ritual that was not mine. I decided it was insurance. I was trying to cover every base in case another calamity befell my dead husband. I finished the words at 11.23 p.m., then said aloud into the silence, 'I'm so sorry, Peter.'

The landline rang. Just once. And stopped. I held my breath, hands motionless under the blanket. Was it a response?

On the forty-ninth morning, I woke to discover the glass doors to the backyard flung open. This was impossible. I was religious about closing everything before bed. They'd been locked against the cold. And yet—forty-nine days.

Who would begrudge those of faith finding or making meaning where they can? Through the interminable winter after he died, I searched for it everywhere. As kids, the nuns taught us to pray for *the grace of a peaceful death*. It was just another baffling set of words to make us squirm before playtime and our free milk, but the prayer resurfaced after Peter died, as I groped for any insight into how to go on.

A friend, wanting to help, gave me a handbook about Jewish rituals.

One of the primary purposes of the mourning customs is to help the mourner(s) find a proper balance between their need to mourn and the necessity that Jewish tradition sees in returning to everyday life.

But without Peter, how could life be 'everyday'? And how could I return to it when he couldn't?

One night, late, I read about the prescribed grieving times for family members: for parents, a year; but for a husband or child, only three months. You can replace them, you see. The book went unopened after that.

Another friend wrote of his understanding of mourning. *We remember in order to honour the person who died. We grieve in order to heal ourselves.* But did I remember Peter accurately? I panicked when I couldn't picture his eyes, hear his voice or conjure his scent, and grieving didn't feel like healing. It felt self-indulgent. I was alive and he was dead; I had the better part of the deal.

The Irish have a tradition of covering up mirrors in a house where there has been a death. That suited me. I pulled on a grey dress on the morning I flew to Melbourne and wore nothing else, other than pyjamas, for months. I wanted to disappear. I understood why widows donned 'weeds'. That plain dark garment allowed me to forget myself and focus on him. It also told the world to look away. Mirrors be damned. I became a shade—which is another word for ghost.

In some cultures, white is worn to mourn, while in others, clothing is ripped or torn. Ecclesiastes tells us: *There is a time to rend and a time to sew.*

(Rend or tend? What a difference a consonant makes, eh, Pete?)

The custom I craved was the black armband, that simple signal that death has visited, and care should be taken.

I'd open his dictionary and flick through, looking for words he had found significant. On page 617, I stumbled over the entry for *grief*: *deep or intense sorrow or mourning.* So that's what the gut-churning, pulse-racing, mouth-drying, brain-addling, eye-burning, bone-wearying emptiness was.

Peter had left no mark anywhere near the word. That was some consolation.

I suppose I was trying to decide *how* to live without him but, more urgently, I wanted reasons *why* to live. I wanted meaning, and eventually it found me in an unexpected place. Despite my scepticism about social media, I'd been an early adopter of Instagram, and one day a friend asked me to post a daily image so she would know I was upright.

Her request woke me to the world, even if only small squares of it. I clicked the orchid against its shadow on the wall; I focused on the red ribbon tied around homegrown jonquils left on the doormat; I framed and reframed the candle's glow against the honeyed surface of the coffee table. Finding beauty for her reminded me I had a responsibility to someone and a promise to keep. Sometimes I wonder why I don't quit Instagram, but it was an anchor then, and today, as I clicked those gulls against the sunset, I remembered how paying attention to the world lifted me out of myself.

Now, I look up, beyond the bat and the palm and the eucalypt, to the dark infinity beyond. Dots of white pierce it, as though there are millions of tiny holes in a dark velvet theatre curtain, the stage lights shining behind.

I'm looking up, Pete. Can you see me?

NEXT MORNING, I SWIM with Marina, grateful that she and I can meet near the edge of our respective five-kilometre cut-off zones. I email friends, asking them to consider donating to a fundraiser for another friend's brother. He and his wife were hiking in a national park in California when a tree branch fell on them. She died instantly and he will never walk again. The winged thing struck from a clear blue sky.

I'm reminded of a story about a little dog that was attacked by an eagle. It escaped, but now, whenever it's outdoors, it runs and sniffs, then stops to check overhead, then runs, then stops to look over its shoulder, then runs. We're all looking over our shoulders for Covid, but forgetting that the feathered predator can take other forms.

For the third time, I cancel the interstate workshop I was to lead. Sometimes, as writing prompts for students, I use images—paintings or photographs—that I've photocopied over and over. Doing this makes certain details loom large while others disappear. That seems to me how memory works. If I catch a fragment and retell it, it becomes more vivid, which makes it feel more real. But are other memories pushed aside as I enlarge the found one?

Recently, my brother Brett reminded me of an afternoon when we were kids. The bailiff was coming to Mum's place, so she put the two of us in the bathroom, along with little Alanna and the TV set, and told us to hide. She must have been terrified, but we thought it was excellent fun.

Or at least that's how I recall him telling me the story. When I checked it with him, he wrote that I'd already misremembered.

> *Not quite how it went . . .*
>
> *Mum stuffed what she could (quite a lot of gear, actually) in the bathroom and when the bailiff came she told you to get in the shower and turn the water on, then warned the bailiff off going in there 'while my daughter is showering'.*
>
> *Can't remember if Alanna was there, or who it was in the bailiff's office that tipped her off, but she knew they were coming and had time to get organised. I remember they took away two old Victa lawnmowers that we'd bought at a garage sale for five bucks each. Ruthless bastards!*

When we raised it with Alanna, she claimed she was the one in the shower and had no memory of us being in the bathroom with her.

I have not a skerrick of recall of that episode, even after being told it twice and rehashing it. I must have been at least twelve at the time. Did I bury the memory because it was upsetting? Or did my seahorses just decide it had to go to make way for something else? Maybe Alanna is right, and I wasn't there. I never got to tell Peter the story, which makes me wonder how many of his memories I didn't get to hear. I'd assumed we knew everything about each other, but I see now how daft that is. We can't even know ourselves fully. In fact, maybe that's the trickiest knowing of all.

And parents? Well, perhaps we can only ever know them through a child's eyes.

The first words most English-speakers say are *Mum* or *Dad*.

As adults, those one-syllable words anchor us to a time when there was always someone to pick you up when you fell or to tell you the way when you were lost.

Mum-mum-mum . . . Dad-dad-dad . . .

Sometimes, now, I say *Dad* with irritation, sometimes with anger or even resentment. Sometimes we bark at each other. I get cross about his smoking or, mortifying as it is to admit, fractious when I want him to give me more attention. Occasionally I rail at him too long because I have the luxury of knowing he will keep on loving me.

Dad called me Bubby right up until Peter's death. Widows age overnight. Mum used to call me Petunia. She was barely more than a child when she gave birth to me and always maintained she was terrified of the small pink bundle she took back to the bush. She was more at home with horses, windmills and mustering, and would fret that I'd die as soon as I went to sleep. She'd wake me, I would scream, and then she'd spend hours crooning 'The Owl and the Pussy-cat'. We danced, me cradled in her arms, by the light of many a moon.

When I was a teenager, she listened to Joni Mitchell—*Ladies of the Canyon* was on high rotation—and joined in with a gravel-voiced bloke who sang of Suzanne going down to a river and birds on a wire. I wished she would listen to classical music or soft jazz, like the other mothers who wore pastels and pearls, not batik or halter-necks. How she'd have smiled to see me queueing for Leonard Cohen concert tickets, decades later. She was fun and unpredictable, and she loved us with a passion that was almost frightening sometimes. We knew no one could hurt us; not while she had breath.

At the age of fifty-seven, Mum lay in a small regional hospital, dying of cancer. She had been told that if she didn't have chemotherapy, she would only survive a year. Resolute, she declined treatment; instead she changed her diet and her days. She refined herself, physically and mentally. I knew, but didn't believe, that we were losing her: the indomitable force that had always made me feel safe on the earth.

For about nine months, she shone, but then she began to dim. Just shy of a year after her diagnosis, she was admitted to hospital. Alanna and I came to be with her after she had said her farewells to Brett. She relaxed, knowing her children were as prepared as they could be. She let me rub moisturiser into her hands and feet and brush her wavy hair. She was no bigger than a twelve-year-old between those stiff white hospital sheets, drifting between places and times. That's when she asked me to sing—something she'd never have requested if not on drugs. I warbled the songs she wanted—'Moon River' and an old hymn about the *star of the sea*—and, in a reversal of roles, I recited 'The Owl and the Pussy-cat'. Now she was tiny and helpless, and I was fixated on her every intake of breath. Alanna and I kept watch in the ghastly duality of wishing her alive while also wishing her the imagined peace of 'gone'. Within a few days, she was. For a long time, the earth felt tremulous underfoot.

Sometimes I wonder if Peter could have known his end was coming. He'd always found the final days of autumn melancholy. He'd sense the creep of his interior darkness rising as tentacles of frost began to clutch at Melbourne's throat. He'd said—remember?—as we walked home from the cinema the weekend before, him blowing into his fingerless gloves, that he didn't want to live through another Melbourne winter.

Was that a kind of magic? Like the way I could wish for Mum to call, from the other side of the continent, and she would? Did he sense the feathered predator, and was that why he told me he loved me at the airport?

———

Here at lockdown central, I cancel yoga classes, a mammogram, a dawn labyrinth walk, a theatre outing and a couple of catch-ups with chums outside the five-kilometre radius. The day becomes a cascade of emails, and I'm glad of the midday distraction of a clattering of sulphur-crested cockatoos. They shriek like rough-voiced hawkers. One large bullyboy lands on the balcony railing, stretching his wings and opening his beak to roar. When I laugh, he pumps up the volume, careening off to the palm tree to protest from a distance. Road rage on the avian highway.

All boxes ticked at the desk, and sun dropping, I stroll, thinking of that snapped branch and the children who are now motherless because of a tree, and of their widower father, paralysed in his grief. I've walked thousands of kilometres under all manner of limbs but have never met a widow-maker.

The city glows like El Dorado across the oily surface of the dark harbour.

Case numbers climb. Deaths, too.

I call Dad; hear him breathe thin whistles of air. I raid the fridge and wash clothes. The cockatoos return, shredding palm leaves, their beaks clacking and ripping. I can see no berries or nuts, even through binoculars. It looks to be nothing more than vandalism. I shout at them, but they ignore me. Back at the computer, I edit then add. It feels as futile as roaring at birds, but it's my work, and I want to make something, so I stay.

Twice a week, at 4 p.m. I join the other members of the Quiet Reading of Books Club. We are four neighbours in this block of flats, sharing books via our milk boxes. On Mondays and Thursdays, we step onto our respective balconies, settling in with a cuppa, and sometimes a beanie or blanket, to read, together apart, for an hour. We began during the first lockdown. I mentioned that one of the things I missed most after Peter died was silent reading in company. Another neighbour said she felt lost without the library. So, we made our own. The birds hush as we enter our fictional worlds. The leaves of the eucalypt hang heavy, inclining towards my pages. At sunset, the sky is grey and shadowy, like the mystery I've been reading.

Days are bookended by walking. It's easy to imagine the world is flat in the mornings, when the sun surfaces and I squint into the *offing*. (Thanks, Pete, for giving me that word for the space between sea and sky on that long-ago summer evening.) One sunset, a plume of spray rises where a rainbow meets the sea. It's as though the colours are solid objects, making a splash in the brine.

Dad jokes that now I'm locked down as well as locked out of the state and locked away from him. He tells me not to worry—the roses have produced three winter blooms, so there's bound to be a beauty waiting when I get there.

We've had to cancel our fortnightly reading-aloud group. Normally, four of us gather to share poems, prose, epics and epigrams, and to discuss the conundrums that arise from them. The loss of these sustaining conversations, and the pleasure of being read to in familiar voices, is sharp.

Conversely, I'm invited to attend Zoom meetings for a trivia night, a card game, writing mornings, meditation group and yoga classes. Virtual life is hectic.

In honour of Peter, I start a list of things to remember . . .

- Zoologist Liz, who never removes her string of seed pearls, even when she swims, tells me the baubles of olive-green seaweed I drape around my neck are *Hormosira banksii*—or Neptune's beads!
- The Chief Medical Officer has a deep frown line on the bridge of her nose. She misreads a word in her report. Has she slept? Is she afraid? Should I be?
- A cloud-whale floats above the unsuspecting tidal station. The sky behind flares like flame, its reflection shimmering across the harbour to my feet. Shepherd's delight.
- A hawk flutters beside me like bunting, so close, on a thermal at the cliff's edge. Something is about to meet its end, but for now it's oblivious to the impending thunderbolt. The breeze ruffles my hair before moving past me to create squall-lines on the sea. I reach to touch the winged thing, but it veers away, westwards.

I give up on the list when, at the press conference to mark the end of the first week, the premier confirms we won't be coming out of lockdown any time soon. For the first time in months, I don't call Dad. I do walk, though. That's non-negotiable.

To cheer myself, I pat every dog I meet and my mood lifts along with the skies. A kestrel holds itself aloft on an updraft, sky-surfing as darkness closes in.

The light is mossy green on the shallows under the Moreton Bay fig. The city appears far, far away. The image is disquieting, but friends comment on how beautiful it is when I post it. In the eye of the beholder, alright.

One week down.

THE WEEKEND RELEASES me from the desk. I walk as fast as I can to my angophora. Its trunk has grown into the shape of a creature's spine; there's a curved rump, a straight back and then a neck that arches up, extending towards the canopy. It's a cross between a horse and a giraffe, with a hide of russet and cream bark. I have been visiting since the second day I arrived here, when it was not much more than a sapling. It's off the path, so I can wrap my arms around it and no human will come past to roll their eyes at us.

Later, I swim with a writer friend who lives up the hill. We celebrate necks and shoulders loosening in the brine and commiserate over lockdown sentences.

At sunset, lurid orange sky fills a puddle. The firmament is at my feet. My runners ripple the heavens.

On Sunday, I chop vegetables. I will make a green soup and a red soup, then portion them into containers for the freezer. In the early years of our marriage, Peter and I discovered we both loved soup-and-toast dinners. It's why I made a vat of minestrone before I left that last time.

After his death, soup was a constant. Borscht, bouillon, chowder, leek and potato, ginger-laced broths, hearty zucchini puree and creamy mushroom—all were left at my front door with notes and flowers. Peter's niece was the maestra of minestrone and my old pal Graeme came bearing vats of chicken soup (aka Jewish penicillin), insisting on helping me squeeze them into the freezer. I understood it was a ploy to check that I was eating. He barely took his eyes off me for a year.

In those first months, the only still point in my days of dealing with banks and telcos, bureaucrats and coroners, of sifting and sorting, and of finding and losing my mind, came as darkness closed in. I would stumble to the refrigerator, extract a container and transfer its contents to a saucepan, then stand over the pot, staring into the heating liquid as though it held answers—to something, anything.

After suitable simmer time, I'd transfer the soup into a bowl and sit. That's when I'd hear the noises—my racing heartbeat; the creak of wooden floorboards as night air entered them; possums skittering along the side fence; wind through the bottlebrushes and the inevitable thrum of rain. Eventually, I'd pick up the spoon.

Soup is invalid fare, meant to heal, but it can burn. It can't be gobbled or rushed. So, I paid attention, blowing on each mouthful to be sure it was safe. I never expected anything of food back then, least of all pleasure. I felt guilty about being alive. And yet . . .

I was unable to ignore the fact that people wanted me to thrive. In that silence at day's end, I tasted their care—the shopping for ingredients, soaking of pulses, reducing of stock, chopping of greens, frying of onions, blending and boiling. Every bowl a labour of love.

Today, as I sauté onions and fennel in olive oil, it occurs to me that just as soup takes time, so too does grief. Back then, I wanted to run at it as if it were the enemy, flinging body and soul against it so I could kill it off as soon as possible. I didn't understand that grief had to become part of me; and, like soup, must to be ingested slowly.

That ritual pause between daytime frenzy and night-time vigilance was one of the things that led me back to life. While grief freezes the spirit, soup can warm it. I gave thanks to whoever had provided and, in doing so, understood why we say 'grace'. That's what I had been delivered, in Tupperware and takeaway containers.

The exhaust fan roars on as the green soup bubbles. Having made a mess of the floor as I cooked, I sprinkle eucalyptus oil into hot water and begin to mop, the job Mum hated most. She would come home, exhausted and aching, from cleaning other people's homes after they'd vacated. Sometimes she'd bring things they'd left behind. A book. A pair of barbecue tongs. A poster. Was that where she got the one in our living room? It was a scarecrow with a helmet and a gun, asking: *What if they gave a war and nobody came?* Of course, I wished for framed prints of European Impressionists, like other kids at school.

What a prat.

I dust the photo of the two of us, taken under an arbour of pink roses in a country garden we visited in the last months of her life. Before Mum died, she gave me a card. In it, she'd written that whenever I saw a pink rose against a sandstone wall, I would know she was close. Dad has two pinks in his sandy strip of blooms.

I dust a photo of Peter, dancing by the edge of Melbourne's bay.

I write and stamp five postcards and letters, then turn off the soup and rug up. After posting the mail, I head for the water's edge. The sky looks liquid, the water flat and solid like a mirror.

I call Dad as I mooch along the sand, telling him I wish I could deliver soup to him, but he's back on song, cooking lamb chops and having a glass or two of white. Besides, he says, his pea and ham is the best, so I couldn't teach him any tricks. I boast that my Sydney Swans beat the West Coast Eagles by ninety-two points. He just laughs—he won't be drawn.

'Thanks for calling, honey,' he says, as he does every time we speak.

In the background, Louis Armstrong is singing Dad's favourite song and the world does seem very wonderful.

'Love you.' He ends every call the same way.

The words I've been writing have eaten the gaps between my vertebrae. My spine clicks with every stride. In nine days, Dad turns ninety-one. I was meant to be flying west tomorrow but my wings have been Covid-clipped.

I will not go under. I will not. But I'm glad of the spiky wind. If I see someone I know, I can say it's the reason for the tears above my mask. Not that we're likely to hang about chatting. Locals step aside on paths and turn from each other on the stairs. Graphs with upward-trending lines dominate the news. Debate rages about vaccinations.

The sky doesn't care and shimmies like a showgirl. It's an end-of-the-world sunset. Memories of the blazes from eighteen months ago lurk near the surface of my lizard brain. We should have been wearing these Covid masks then, for protection against the fumes.

It was high summer, and the skies boiled for weeks. I photographed them as my lungs filled with smoke and humidity-created mould. I exercised in my flat with the windows closed, dancing on tiptoe so as not to disturb the neighbours. I shut doors and shut my mouth—thousands had it so much worse—but I couldn't shut out the screams of koalas, their flesh singed and burning, on the evening news. Friends huddled in emergency meeting places or helped neighbours to escape. The Pilgrim worried for his octogenarian sister, sleeping in her car with her dog and photo albums, while the country's leader holidayed in Hawaii.

I developed a thick cough and was sent for lung tests, sucking in air and pushing it out, holding it and sucking again. The technician asked why I was crying. I said it was tired eyes, but the truth was that with each inhalation I pictured the charry residue on my balcony railings, remembered Dad telling me how frightened he was when emphysema got the better of him, and felt the clutch in my chest, just like when I swim and the dark shape comes at me. The technician had to count me towards calm . . . *ten, nine, eight . . . breathe . . . seven, six, five, nearly done . . .*

Now, down at the Cove with the Pilgrim, I remember I dreamed I was underwater in a car. Headlights cut yellow ribbons through water that swirled like smoke. My hands slipped on the wheel, as though I were trying to hold a fish. Charred fragments of roof lining floated around the car's interior.

I don't share the story.

The sky inflames above the weatherboard tidal station. Two children seated on the gangway lean towards each other, as if reassuring themselves the inferno overhead holds no malice.

'Apocalyptic beauty,' I whisper.

The Pilgrim doesn't hear me, but I don't repeat myself. That sky commands silence.

———

Life blurs in the daily routine of meditation, walk to wake the body, swim to rinse off gloom, desk, press conference, desk, sunset, repeat. Covid deaths soar. I sense, in some reporting, that while the old are counted, they don't really count. I worry about Dad and the Old Salt and the Pilgrim, and my octogenarian swimmers and Zoologist Liz, who I've not spotted for ages.

On the cliff path, a man called Jez tells me he's homeless. He has a dog, though, and he keeps her nice. Everyone needs someone to look after, he reckons. Some bloke offered him money for her a couple of days back, but you don't sell your mates. It's hard, Jez says, because no one carries cash now, with the plague, so he rarely gets a night in a hostel to sort and repack his belongings, and to shower. Says he doesn't cope when Mitzi gets hungry. You can't explain this Covid shit to a dog.

Jez began walking further afield when the lockdowns started. No one in the city. And besides, he's not bound by a five-kilometre limit if he hasn't got an address. Home isn't where you are but who you're with, he reckons, and Mitzi is family. Better than the one he got born into. So they duck and weave, duck and weave. He's a tortoise, lumbering with his pack on his back. Mitzi wears a scarf and licks my hand.

It's over a fortnight since I saw Lucien Henry's waratah painting. What happens to artworks without eyes alighting on them? Do curators whisper to them, like keepers in a wildlife sanctuary?

The surf is way up. There are boardriders in the harbour. When I swim, the swell lifts me high, like I'm a bird on an updraft, before lowering me onto the sand where the net was lying only a month ago. Can that be?

The clouds are serene as they float westwards. A welcome swallow dips into the water, rises, dips again. You're so welcome, little bird.

During the Quiet Reading of Books hour, a butcherbird visits Neighbour Margie's balcony. I've seen them rip into the flesh of another bird with as much gusto as a falcon, their hooked beaks as precise as scalpels, but this one sits very still, a grey-and-black sentinel, watching her read. Then it tilts its head to sing, trilling and thrilling us, reminding us not to judge a book by a cover or a bird by its feathers.

Afterwards, I stay on the balcony, rugged up, watching a sliver of crescent moon float across the clearest of skies. I leave it for the interminable semifinal of *MasterChef*.

Next evening, inky wisps colonise the sky, merging to make the shape of a black swan, which is the bird emblem of Western Australia. I take it as a sign to call Dad. He reminds me there used to be a pond at Perth airport and a family of swans lived on it. There was a bar, too.

'It was called the Orbit Inn. We would go out sometimes on Sunday afternoons to have a beer while we watched the planes from the observation deck,' he says. 'Remember?'

Family and friends came to farewell me when I first flew out of the country at the age of twenty-one. I was dressed for flight—back then we put on our finest—and everyone else was smart in 'Sunday best'. Travel was adventure—even for those who waited on the deck, waving as the plane taxied away.

I'm thrilled with this memory from Dad. It's like a jigsaw piece clicking into place. I can't wait to remind Alanna, who is already watching the *MasterChef* grand final as it labours on. We text about brie ice cream, which just sounds blah, but the dish is made by a contestant called Justin—my younger brother's name—so it's a triumph when he wins. We don't know as we applaud that the cheeky Scottish judge, our adored favourite who laughs easily and empathises instantly, will die suddenly and alone just two years later—or that we will grieve as if he were our own.

The day before Dad's birthday, Sonia visits him, bringing a bottle of white and a handful of scratchies. She and I were at high school together and grew up in each other's families. Her clan is French Mauritian, so I got extracurricular language lessons, although much of what was said might not have been helpful in an exam. I'd go with them to the river for crabbing expeditions, singing and dancing in the dark, led by her vivacious mother, who has been in a nursing home for years now, her effervescent personality damped down by dementia. She still smiles and winks, but words left her long ago. Sonia visits her almost daily, taking chopped mango, prawns and bananas for her ma to devour, which she does, with relish.

Dad adores Sonia. Everyone does, including her husband, Les. They've been together since they were sixteen. Dad is chuffed—*almost as good as seeing you, darling*—and is off to scratch his tickets over a glass of wine. The lucky man is in top form.

Outside, clouds loom. I wobble, thinking of Dad and Sonia together. But a ray of light sneaks through, and the harbour catches and reflects it. Glory be, I whisper, before returning for Zoom meditation group—thirty or more of us in our darkened squares. One of the regulars is in Japan, reporting on the out-of-cycle Olympics. It's sweltering there, he says. I touch my toes to my hot-water bottle, listen to the even tones coming through the speakers, and close my eyes.

And Dad turns ninety-one.

I make a video and email it to Justin, so he can play it to Dad. I wear a navy-and-white-striped turtleneck under a navy jumper. With my short hair and scrubbed face, I resemble a nun. Well, I'm living a cloistered life. I post a picture on Instagram: me and Dad with his red roses. It was taken in December, when last I saw him. It has been seven months.

Afterwards, I potter towards sunset at Pilgrim pace, and we're rewarded with the biggest sky in weeks. The headland has shrunk to Lego size, and the white lighthouse is a Monopoly token. Clouds drift, like monumental golden jellyfish, their tentacles drooping almost to the sea. They are harbingers, sent by great wild deities; reminders that all of us, with our viruses and lockdowns and sanitisers, are insignificant, and even the mightiest ocean can be trumped by sky. These are cumulus for kings. Happy birthday, Dad. What a cake.

The Pilgrim poses a favourite question: *Do I think the universe is on my side, disinterested or malevolent?* I ponder, but I feel so engulfed in the world for this fleeting moment, so much a part of it, that the question makes no sense. It's like asking if I am on my own side—although sometimes the answer to that might be an emphatic no. But today I'm clear that although I'm an insignificant speck, I belong to this majesty. There are no sides and no separation. I can't answer his question. He doesn't mind; he's busy trying to find extra puff for the uphill home.

Later, I FaceTime with the Perth family. Dad says, *Cheers, darling*, and lifts his glass, exposing purple bruises like storm clouds on his hand and arm.

Melbourne starts its sixth lockdown. Not knowing whether to sympathise or stay silent, I go to the clifftops. Thick black clouds make me speed, head down, into the wind. Looking up on cue, I locate a patch of blue with three defiantly upright palms framed against it. I snap them for Instagram, and underneath I write that it's Friday. An old friend comments that it has been Saturday all day, and I'm not sure who is right.

Next day, it's definitely Saturday. My phone alarm reminds me to log on, and I set up at the dining table for a session with my sisters and our friend Louise. We have been holding a 'Zoom Art Day' every month or so for a year now. It started during the first Melbourne lockdown, when they couldn't meet as normal at Alanna's place.

We chat, then sink into cross-border silence. We're together apart, working with what is to hand—coloured pencils or textas, sometimes crayons—and drifting in and out of talk and tea. I have four tubes of glitter paint and use the red and yellow to create a Shark Beach sunset. I've no need of blue or green.

I want to apologise to them, as though I'm the furniture removalist who crossed the border illegally like an invading starling, returning Covid to them along with carpet rolls and faded armchairs, but we work without comment.

When I go to greet the real sunset, it's mellow yellow, but the wind buffets and shoves, the sea chops and spits. I photograph a lone pine against a supersized sky.

Lisa downstairs, who regularly has magpies visiting her kitchen, made a sign for her door: a rainbow, with the phrase *Andrà tutto bene* written above it. As I take my washing down to the laundry, I hum it to myself.

All will be well. All is okay . . .

At sunset, the world is grey, like the feather of a dove. I walk into the dark, before scurrying home to set up on the sofa for Trivia Zoom. The collective noun for flamingos is *flamboyance*. (Who knew, Pete?)

In the small hours, I wake, asphyxiating, my mouth full of paper, gagging as I try to spit it out. I turn on the bedside light, stand, wobble, and kick my little toe on the pine trunk near the bedroom door, then stub my big toe on the side table.

'Owwww.' Tears. So immediate. Instant.

In the study, I fling open the top drawer of my desk, oblivious to the teenage girl sleeping below. I rummage—dropping pens, scattering prescriptions, grabbing at cables and the hole punch—until I find it. Peter's list.

I return to bed, read for a couple of hours, then tuck the envelope between the pages of a poetry collection. I meditate. The sun rises. I walk and swim, heart still racing, and as soon as it is late enough, I make the calls.

My father is steady, both my brothers assure me.

My sisters in Melbourne remind me they know how to weather lockdowns. I begin to slow, to notice the snail tattoo on my finger, and at day's end I've snared twelve hundred words. Don't look back at them, I warn myself.

On the stairs, I see Lisa's sign. *Andrà tutto bene.* My feet thrum the words. I want spells and sorcery; an incantation to make things better. Overhead, a hawk hovers, buoyed by thin air, holding its position against the sea spray. I leave it there, wishing that my peregrines would hurry up and arrive on their Melbourne scrape so I can watch them on their webcam, but instead I convene via Zoom with the reading-aloud group members. We've accepted we can't do without a dose of Dante, so we read to each other from inside digital squares. It's a balm to be back.

Four weeks, I tell Dad when he asks how long it has been. I wish I could send him the images of my sunsets, but instead, today, I try to describe it for him. Fishing boats bob before a burning horizon. Backlit fig leaves, like a lace mantilla, frame the image I snap.

A *mantilla*, Dad. Like a veil . . .

He laughs. Why would he need to know that word?

It was obvious from today's press conference that we're not getting out of lockdown, lockup, lockout, any time soon. I just exhaled and kept working. Acceptance is not resignation, as I've learned from Dad.

A month of homestay ends with a job in a recording studio near Sydney Uni. We may leave our five-kilometre boundary for employment, so I wake the car. Driving at fifty kilometres per hour is a rush. My seahorses dance as I recall the same sensation from years ago. I'd been walking in Spain for weeks— thirty- and forty-kilometre slogs through tough terrain—when a man gave me a lift. I was giddy with speed, until the driver apologised that he could only do forty kilometres per hour because his van was so old.

In the studio, I remove my mask, sanitise hands and edge into the booth, slipping back into professional life behind a microphone, relishing the privilege of work. The scripts advertise protection against hail, flood, fire and earthquake— laughable to imagine we can insure against the winged thing.

Afterwards, I visit my GP for a second Covid vaccination. I've relied on him to be my sounding board since I moved here—he's like the tree at the centre of a forest, keeping an ecosystem alive—but today he's weary. He and his staff have been abused, just for asking patients to wear masks.

Back inside my five kilometres, I stop the car to pay my respects to a mammoth Moreton Bay fig, its bark a pitted hide. I lean into it, skin on skin, and imagine it roaming the cliffs at night. A dervish, whirling.

I drive home, put the car back to sleep, change into soft clothes and head for the water. The sky is palest chiffon blue, with barely a horizon line. There's nothing in the offing.

SPREAD-EAGLED, I LET the water take me. This current will swirl out to Bottle and Glass Point, passing Parsley Bay's white swing bridge, rippling on beyond the ferry wharf at Watsons Bay, with its old wooden fishermen's cottages and new glass mansions, dodging Sow and Pigs Reef, to tickle the toes of toddlers near the tidal station at Camp Cove. Then it will slide by the nude bathers at Lady Jane before finally melding into the Pacific Ocean, just below the red and white stripes of the Hornby Lighthouse. For now, I go with its flow inside the net. I'm flotsam.

Or am I jetsam?

Peter would want me to decide. Flotsam and jetsam are different, he explained one day at Aireys Inlet, as we walked barefoot along the wide strip of shiny sand towards the red-capped lighthouse. Both words describe marine debris, he said, but flotsam is for stuff that goes overboard by accident—materials from a shipwreck or mishap, like the recent container-load of disposable nappies. I can't imagine sea creatures would be comforted knowing that was accidental. Jetsam, on the other hand, is debris that's intentionally dumped, most often to lighten a ship's load. It's a shortening of the word jettison, while the word flotsam derives from the French word *flotter*, to float.

So yes, I must be flotsam. I'm floating here by a series of accidents; coincidences and serendipities that washed me up on this shore like a piece of sea glass . . .

Four months after Peter died, on the twentieth anniversary of my mother's death, I flew to Sydney. I was to take part in the opening ceremony for a sandstone and bluestone labyrinth in Centennial Parklands. A collection of elders and faith leaders had been invited to walk it, infusing it with blessings or wishes. I was to represent 'unaligned pilgrims'—those who walk without claiming a faith tradition. I placed my feet on the stone, not knowing what to expect or what to do. It wound me in and out of myself, backwards and forwards in time, through conscious and unconscious, as I wished and hoped, trying to focus on those whose feet would come after, but worried I had no powers.

I'm never sure what prayer is, but that day I prayed with my soles. I offered steps for Peter and Mum, but also for those to come, who might tread the labyrinth's brain-shaped path. Afterwards, I was shaken by the experience. I excused myself and strolled downhill, in spring sweetness, through grimy streets and past empty shops, towards my old inner-city neighbourhood. I was literally unsettled, looking for something to tether me, so I set a course for the flat that had been mine when I first met Peter. I wanted to catch a glimpse of the woman I had been pre-him. Near Rushcutters Bay Park, where he asked me to marry him just two months after we met, I wandered, half in the now and half in then. Focused on the contrast between the electric blue of the sky and the neon green of the jacaranda canopy, I almost tripped on an OPEN FOR INSPECTION sign in front of a dark brick building from the 1930s.

I'd often fantasised about those apartments. In fact, I was writing a story set in them—the same story that had taken me out to the seaside cemetery the day before Peter died. The protagonist, a woman called Ellen, lived in my imagined interior of the building. Her apartment was the first thing I'd 'seen' when I began to write; it was almost empty, painted white. The floors were polished boards, and a narrow balcony ran along the front of the living area, looking onto a eucalypt and a mature palm tree. I was very specific about that; Ellen spent hours observing those two trees and their winged inhabitants.

Clearly, I had to inspect the flat. Perhaps it could be home? Perhaps I could go back in time and pick up threads from my previous life, maybe rewrite history.

Inside, it was just me and a real estate agent called Nick. My disappointment must have been obvious. The carpets and walls were dark, the windows hung with maroon velvet. There was a balcony but no trees. Nick asked what kind of place I wanted. I told him I wasn't really looking; that it was nostalgia for the life I'd had around the corner; that this building was the site of a story I was writing; that I was wasting his time; that I wasn't sure where I wanted to live; that I was sorry; that I was rambling; that my husband had died—

'Oh,' he said. 'Then you have no idea who you are, do you?'

That stopped me.

Nick told me that when his dad died, his mother had been literally lost.

'If you decide to move back to Sydney,' he said, 'I'll find you a home.'

'Don't be daft.'

'No. I watched Mum. She would never have been able to find a place on her own. I'll do the same for you if you come north.'

I shook my head. Yeah, sure.

'It'll be okay,' he said. 'You'll make it home.'

Making a home anywhere seemed unimaginable, but somehow this stranger with the confident manner and X-ray vision managed to cut through. Nick kept checking in, and over the ensuing months, as I packed up in Melbourne and realigned myself towards Sydney, he guided me. He asked the right questions—and not just about real estate. When I got to Sydney, he was waiting. He berated me when I was naive about a property and straight-talked when I got sucked into fantasy. He refused to bid for me when I was likely to 'do my dough'. He stayed the distance on the worst days, edging me towards the future with a combination of bluntness, humour and compassion.

Friends were aghast. 'You're taking advice from a Sydney real estate agent?'

But Nick steered me through indecision and desperation. We saw dozens of possible homes, and when I grew worn down by the search, the rising prices and the shysters, he counselled me to take a break; to stay on at Amanda's place and rest.

That was not going to work. I was sleeping in the room in which I'd made all those phone calls to Peter. For me, it was where he had died. Every night I lay there, chasing sleep and remembering the sounds of *Call the Midwife* from the next room, and the five words our doctor neighbour had spoken. That 'Oh . . .'

Eventually, I decided to quit hunting and rent. But two days later, Nick called to tell me to drive out to the very tip of the harbour, near the cliffs that form its entrance.

'Are you crazy?' I said. 'It's way too far.'

'Just do it,' he said.

So, because this was Nick and he had driven all over town for me, I did.

I pulled up outside a cream-brick building, squat and unprepossessing, on a main road. It had an old frangipani in the front garden, but no personality. Charmless, I thought, although maybe I said it aloud, because Nick shook his head and ushered me forward.

'Wait,' he said, as we climbed to the second floor where, expecting nothing, I followed him through a dark grey door.

The flat was white, save for one wall the colour of the dust of my childhood. Polished floors glowed. I could see it all in a single sweep of my eyes. There was nothing hidden; no surprises. When I stepped onto the narrow balcony, I was almost bowled over by two lorikeets—rainbow-coloured missiles—whizzing along their thoroughfare of air. In their wake, I gasped. I could almost touch a tall overhanging eucalypt and beside it—could it really be?—a palm tree.

It was mine by the end of the week. Hand shaking, I signed the sale contract, with Nick there to steady me. This was late on Easter Thursday: season of death and resurrection. On Good Friday, I walked the neighbourhood as bells from the two churches across the road tolled in different keys. One was called Star of the Sea; that was the name of the bluestone church around the corner from us in Melbourne. The other was—is—St Peter's.

I discovered the red-and-white-striped lighthouse out at the farthest point of the headland. As I stood beside it, watching waves break over tessellated rocks and seabirds dipping in the spray, I thought about angels, light and dark. People use words like 'numinous' and 'spirituality'. They talk of transcendence, destiny and fate. I don't know if I have faith, yet I touch wood, like some ancient Celt, hoping tree-gods might hear, and I whisper incantations to stars and sunsets; to the God of candlelit chapels and frankincense; to the protectors and harbingers of my childhood, with their feathered wings and feet; to patron saints of back roads and pilgrims; and to all those who've gone before. Maybe their atoms were swirling around me out there. Maybe they sent me to the labyrinth that day, or maybe they sent Nick. There are stranger things.

Under the lighthouse, on a day that commemorates a crucifixion, I gave thanks for the unearned luck I'd been granted—another word for it might be *grace*. Six weeks later, I was handed the keys to my new home. I woke there for the first time exactly one year to the day after Peter's death.

I've drifted into the centre of the semicircle of safety, back in the here and now. On the shoreline, Marina collects plastic while Ranger John drives his mini-jeep from bin to bin along the boardwalk. The coffee clutch congregates in front of the Covid-closed kiosk, standing apart but talking up a storm after their laps.

When I arrived here, I worried my story would leak like blood, staining every encounter with grief—or, worse, that death might be contagious, like a virus, and that I might infect others. I wanted to leave the story behind; not have it precede me, as it did in Melbourne. Eventually, I told a few people, but no one fussed. Most regulars are in their eighth or ninth decade, and all have known loss. Some have swum here daily for decades, and they never shy away from that taboo word: *old*.

'Ageing is for wine,' said the Old Salt one morning as we showered under the branches of a dark-trunked tuckeroo. 'And lord knows, I'm partial to a drop. But I'm bloody old, and I don't mind saying so. Better than the alternative.'

'You wouldn't want to be young again?'

'Sure I would, kid. In a heartbeat. But the only choice I've got is old or dead, so I'm making the most of what's on offer, and I'm keeping the hell out of the way of this virus. I reckon this beach is the safest place.'

After discovering the Hornby Lighthouse that first Easter, it became my safe place. My daily ritual, then, was to leave home before dawn and hightail it out to South Head. I'd sit on the grass, tucked against the red and white stripes, gazing across two kilometres of open water to North Head.

The high sandstone headlands at the harbour entrance have been sentinels for millennia. Like the original inhabitants, they've seen the arrival of settlers and convicts, refugees, tourists, developers, conservers, Spanish influenza and Covid-19. Over on North Head sits the Quarantine Station. Opened in the 1830s, it was operational until 1984 when, presumably, it was thought redundant. It's now a luxury hotel.

Every morning, I'd wait by the Hornby for the sun to heave itself from the water. Some things don't change, I'd tell myself, as dawn rays turned the sandstone face of the headland opposite from beige to peach.

See? Same as always; same as ever.

Then, one morning, the unthinkable. Great sections of North Head had sheared off in the night. I blinked, squinting and refocusing, as though my eyes were playing a trick. But no. There it was: a wound on the enduring one; absence where there had been a glowing presence. I gasped, like a fish out of water, or my darling father in the dread dead of night. Not possible. Surely.

What a bird brain. Would I never learn? Things fall and keep falling. Tectonic plates keep shifting.

I'm floating near the net when a white cockatoo shrieks, calling me back. Another follows it, and another, and now there's a flock directly overhead. They wheel and squeal in furious, squawking disagreement, and then, as though of one mind, they turn, pirouetting like a strident corps de ballet as glimmers of sun catch their undersides. They re-form into a flower before fanning out again into a ballooning cloud shape.

'Look, Pete,' I whisper. 'Sky-dancing.'

Just like the fish I saw earlier, weaving below me, the birds appear choreographed. This is a school of cockatoos; that was a murmuration of whiting.

Peter taught me that word one August evening as hundreds of

starlings swirled above the Seine, their reflection an undulating smudge on the great river's surface.

'A murmuration,' he whispered.

It was my first trip to Paris. We were celebrating our eighteenth wedding anniversary. Old hands had warned us about visiting the capital in summer—stifling heat, residents fled, nothing to see—but the days were benign, made for cycling and strolling in T-shirts and broad-brimmed hats, and the nights were balmy, with echoes bouncing off cobbles as we flâneured through extended dusks.

That particular, pink-tinged evening, we were leaning over the railings of the Pont de l'Archevêché, waiting for one of the long, open-topped tourist boats to drift below. We'd splurged on roses at a market so we could drop them down to passengers on the outdoor deck. It felt imperative to share our good fortune.

As we watched the boat cruising towards us, Peter pointed out that there'd once been a morgue only metres from where we were standing. It was built in 1804 on the Île de la Cité, just behind Notre-Dame Cathedral, to house the bodies of those drowned in the Seine. The morgue became a major tourist attraction, drawing thousands of people each day to gawp at the corpses, to see and be seen. It was a kind of gallery, though the writer Émile Zola called it a theatre, where crowds applauded cadavers. It existed for a century before being closed for reasons of 'moral hygiene'. We were amused by that phrase, impervious to the possibility that a morgue could one day house us.

The boat was beneath us, so we dropped the flowers one by one, excitement on the upturned faces making it worth every euro cent. As we turned to follow the boat's progress, I asked Peter about the location of the nets that had been strung across the river to catch corpses for the morgue, but he was distracted. The starlings had returned and were wheeling and whirling above us.

'I think murmuration might be the loveliest word I know,' he said, 'but it doesn't get a listing in my dictionary.'

He was right. Back in Melbourne, we double-checked. It was a spectacular oversight, but as Pete said, dictionaries reflect the biases of their compilers, so some beauty will inevitably be excluded. And, of course, not all knowledge is in books, despite what Mr Arthur Mee would have had me believe.

Around the time I started school, Mum and my step-father scraped together the money to buy Mr Mee's famous *Children's Encyclopaedia*. Perhaps they bought it on subscription, because my memory is that the collection of maroon hardbacks, with their embossed gold lettering, grew over time. Ordered alphabetically, they held a whole world that stretched far beyond the boundaries of our post-and-wire fence lines. I had no idea—I don't think Mum did either—that there was a hierarchy of knowledge, or more 'reputable' encyclopedias. I just sat, cross-legged and open-mouthed, taking in wonders and seeking meaning. Now, I get the same thrill when I spot a new creature on the sea floor.

The cockatoos have gone. I dive under but the fish have scarpered too. Surfacing, I spot Marina's blue cap. She's back in the water, down at the other end. I've never told her about the Parisian nets strung to catch bodies, because I don't want to admit to the crawling sensation in my gut when I accidentally touch our net underwater. It's as though it's alive and could twist around me, squeezing the breath from me—yet I've seen it, flaccid and harmless on the sand, when we look for seahorses. I need to think of it as a haven for me and the hippocampi, so I put my head down and swim as fast as I can, occasionally taking in a gulp of salt water. It stings my sinuses and throat, but it won't do me any harm, as Esme would have said.

Some mornings, I'd watch her carer, a slight girl in thin cotton trackpants, lug a black bucket up the concrete steps from the beach. Esme had cancer.

'It won't kill me,' she told me. 'But there's no fixing me either.'

She couldn't swim anymore. Scabs marked her face and hands. She missed the salt water, so her carer brought it to her. Sometimes, the bucket was for her legs—she'd lower a shin into it and stand, twitching at the bite of brine. Other times, the bucket was placed between the handles of her walking frame so she could plunge her face in, holding her breath in the silky darkness. When she emerged, her thin grey hair dripped, and the scabs were softer.

'This beach is populated by widows,' she said to me once. I'd never told her I was a widow, but after that I saw others in their black togs with fresh eyes.

She died just before her 101st birthday; an elder, gone from us. I was away hiking at the time. On my return, I slid into the harbour and stroked through my salty sorrow. It's impossible to cry underwater.

Or is it, Pete?

Do fish cry? You told me they experience pain, and also have some memory. Can they comprehend a forever absence? Do they grieve?

Keep breathing. Keep stroking. Stay here. Stay now.

I scan the harbour floor for a little ray or a flathead—or if I'm lucky, as I once was, a small octopus, tripping along on its tentacles. But there's no movement except the drift of white sand into creamy sand. It's a submerged Sahara, unaffected by surface conditions. A flock of gulls flies over, casting shadows on the watery dunes. I am a dark blur, stroking across a drowned desert.

The first summer I ventured into harbour water, fish spooked me, and I'd stop swimming at every sighting. Then I'd push myself to start again, counting every stroke as I strained to reach one hundred.

When I swam into autumn, I began to relax, managing a lap without stopping. I told myself that if I didn't flee from winged things in the air, there was no need to baulk at a finned thing in the water. I saw toadfish as starlings of the sea and noted how the speedy yellowtails mimicked racing lorikeets. Still, I kept counting. It had become a pacifying mantra.

Some of the regular swimmers learned my name and egged me on. I began to really see them, too.

The Old Salt had a brown birthmark on his upper thigh, a red keloid gash down the centre of his chest and dark sunspots on his balding head. He also had a son in jail, and when he told me about him, he pulled his cap down and turned away.

Grey hairs curled at the Breaststroke Queen's crotch, just above where the carcinoma was removed. Once, as I was helping her out of the water in a big swell, she gripped my hand and hissed, 'I thought the fucker was going to get me this time.' We stood in the shallows, panting and laughing, as waves slapped her thigh with its tell-tale stitch marks.

A *scar* is a wound that has healed. I know that from page 1292 of Peter's dictionary. The word also has a second meaning.

The lasting effect of grief etc. on a person's character or disposition

Most of the regulars are familiar with both definitions, and our bared flesh creates intimacies. We say we wouldn't know each other with clothes on. We drop our guards along with our towels, sharing confidences before surnames. There's always a joke, and mostly they're corny.

'I've come down for my hit of Vitamin Sea.'

Humour as painkiller . . .

Zoologist Liz donated a kidney to her then ten-year-old daughter, who went on to live another twenty-three years. Now, Liz tends the hedge of rosemary on her darling's grave and encourages me to pick sprigs for my roast vegetables whenever I walk uphill to the cemetery at day's end. It's small, but clamours with stories. After I gather the sharp-smelling herb, I harvest names from tombstones. Prudence, Charity and Honour. Winsome and Euphemia, Hattie and Elsie—my grandmother Ning's name. Most aren't heard now. Names also die.

Liz doesn't swim in winter. I suspect Peter would hibernate, too. His toes were always frozen, and it's hard for me to imagine him leaping from a warm bed to fling his body into icy water. But, then, it's hard to imagine anything of how he'd be now, just as it's impossible to picture my mother, who would be the Old Salt's twin, at eighty-three. They are stilled lives.

That first aquatic year, as winter made its presence felt, I grew apprehensive about continuing to swim. Chilly days were tied to tea dregs and vomit-stained sheets. I'd wake, convinced by something at the edge of my dream-vision that the winged creature was returning, and I didn't want to stare down anything dark. But the regulars joshed me into staying.

'You're not going to pike, are you, kid?'

The 'kid' took the bait, persuading Marina, who was also considering a winter pause, that the icy winds weren't so bad. Flinging ourselves in, we declared the glacial water good for our innards. I counted more and more strokes, speeding up to keep my blood moving. We bought cheap towelling dressing-gowns, black for her and white for me, and when we finished our whooping laps, we shed our togs and wrapped our naked selves in them, looking for all the world like oversized toddlers.

Trying to fathom who to be, I cut my long hair short—it was easy to wash, easy to dry, easy to tuck under a swim cap.

The risen sun is in my eyes as I stroke the last lap. Time to move into the day: the beach shower; breakfast with a pandemonium of parrots; then the blank, unruly page. The reward for sticking with it will be to call Dad, but I must be patient. It's still only 5 a.m. where he is.

At day's end, I will walk with the Pilgrim, who is shrinking from the radiotherapy. He can't taste food; can't make saliva. Sometimes it's as though he's behind a glass wall, in the world but also removed from it. I worry the exertion will be bad for him, but he texted that sunset and moonrise will be simultaneous this evening and he wants to get up to the cliffs to observe the planets dancing.

I wish Dad could see them too. I wish I could lower him into this salty water and let it hold him, as it does me. I am so fortunate to have washed up on this shore—and I've been swimming all this time without having counted a single stroke.

'GOT TIME FOR a yarn?' asks the Old Salt, as we shower under dark-trunked tuckeroos. It's rare for him to make a request, so after drying off, I sit beside him on the concrete seawall—perhaps not the requisite 1.5 metres, but definitely distanced—watching a pair of yellow-tailed black cockatoos circling over the net. Their wails echo around the curve of sand.

'*Zanda funerea*,' he says.

'Sorry?'

'That's their name—supposedly because they look like they're going to a funeral. Hopefully it won't be their own, poor buggers. They shouldn't be here in the city at all.'

They flap languorously—mournfully, even—across the water, heading for Chowder Bay. Then, near the marker at Sow and Pigs Reef, they wheel about, their slow-motion flaps easing them towards us. They're in no rush to start the serious work of the day either.

'Must've flown over from Centennial Park.'

'Ah.'

'Enjoy them while you can, kiddo. They're not round much these days.'

I wave to the Elegant Backstroker as she completes her kilometre. The Old Salt is silent. His focus is still on the birds.

'My dad was a cocky—that's what the rich farmers used to call the little blokes, you know. Cockies.'

The water is glossy. There's not the faintest breeze to ruffle its surface, only the vee spreading out from the Backstroker's toes. A psychotherapist, she once told me old age is a gradual *ascent* into unknowing.

A kookaburra lands on the grass. Its beak pierces the surface, emerging with a worm, which it chug-a-lugs down before lifting off again. A nearby magpie cocks its head left, right, then hops away. It's the quick and the hungry here.

'What do you call a flathead in a tuxedo?' the Old Salt asks.

Flummoxed, it takes me a moment to realise it's a joke. 'Dunno,' I manage finally.

'So-fish-ticated!'

'Oh, that's your worst ever.' I laugh, and my hippocampi wriggle, locating a prize. 'I've got one for you,' I say.

'Well, that's a turn-up. Go on.' He shuffles closer to hear better.

'I'm not much chop at jokes,' I warn him.

'Don't make excuses before you begin. First rule of comedy.'

'Well, a friend told this at Peter's wake. She said she remembered him telling it to her when she was playing my kid sister, when we were acting together . . .'

'Too much preamble. Just tell it.'

So I dive in, hearing Peter's voice as a base layer with my friend's alto harmonising. I try to catch their cadences—his enjoyment of the original, and then her retelling it, so unexpectedly, as mourners in funeral blacks stood in a wooden hall, juggling tea, sandwiches, sorrow and party pies, among hay bales and checked tablecloths and posies in Mason jars, making a country-show arvo-tea scene that Peter would have loved. And my friend stepped up . . .

'There's this actor, walking along a beach, waiting for his agent to call. He sees a bottle and picks it up. Rubs it, of course. He knows the drill. And a genie appears. The genie tells him he can have three wishes. Anything he'd like.

'The actor thinks for a moment. Anything? He should go big. "Right then. No more wars, genie. World peace, please."

'The genie winces. "Mate, I really want to give you what you want, but that's way outside my remit. Sorry. Have another go."

'So the actor looks deep into the bottle and eventually nods. "Okay. I'd like to reverse global warming. Let's have leaders agree the science is real and work together while there's still time."

'The genie shakes his head. "Easy, tiger. I'm no god. You'll have to think again. And choose carefully. It's your last shot."

'The actor walks to the water's edge, the genie trailing behind as the sun sinks low. Finally, the actor speaks. "Okay, I've got it. I'd like to be offered a challenging role in a beautiful play, with a cast of actors I admire, directed by someone I respect, with a long rehearsal period, earning a dignified salary."

'The genie stares out to sea. Finally, he turns to the actor. "Hmm," he says. "How about we have another go at world peace?"'

The Old Salt doesn't laugh. Not even a polite chuckle. Maybe he didn't hear properly. Maybe it was my delivery. Maybe—

'I'm sorry about your bloke,' he says. 'I shouldn't have said that about the birds—that they're named for funerals. Sorry, kid.'

I want to tell him it's fine, that it wasn't the birds or their plumage. I want to explain it was pleasure to tell a piece of the story I'd forgotten; how the joke had helped, and how just for a moment that bleak day felt almost ordinary, our grief suspended in the release of corpsing, but all I can do is reach across to touch his hand.

'I'm good. Really. I'm all good.'

Our occasional near-nakedness under neighbouring showers doesn't translate to intimacy, so I don't let my hand linger—and besides, Covid—but an agreement has been reached and we sit, watching a lone Pacific gull. If I can't be with Dad, observing his mischief of magpies, this will do. An eddy of air shivers across the surface towards us, prickling my damp scalp.

The Old Salt chuckles. 'How about we have another go at world peace?'

The cockatoos flap towards Bottle and Glass Point, sky-swimmers in widow's togs. They call—*keeee-owwww*—as they crest the ridge, mourners on the wing.

'Suppose we should make tracks too,' the Old Salt says.

He stands, holding out his hand, and as I take it, he thanks me. 'For staying. You know, for company. I know you're busy, but it was good to sit for a minute, kid.'

I should admit there's nothing I'll do today that will be as important as this hiatus, watching those birds and listening to the pauses between our words. I could tell him how time is doing strange things through this lockdown—racing and slowing, stretching and bending—and, like him, I'm probably alone too much, and how this moment we've spent together will sustain me for hours. I could try to explain that lockdown reminds me of my first widow-weeks, or that he reminds me of a sturdy version of my father, but he has hoisted his frayed canvas beach bag and is efforting up the stairs. I fall in behind then beside him. Our pace is funereal, but it doesn't feel sad.

'If you could have a wish,' he says, eyes straight ahead, 'would you ask the genie to bring him back?'

I'm shocked. We don't normally go to such personal places. 'It's hard,' I say. 'I don't know if we'd fit anymore. I don't know if I want anyone now, not even him.' I don't know what to say. To feel . . .

The Old Salt stops. He's panting, but it isn't that.

'I'm sorry, kid,' he says. 'I'm a bloody old fool.' He does look old then; and small. 'I wish I could fix things . . .'

'No, it's a good question,' I say. 'But I don't have an answer.'

I remember what Real Estate Agent Nick said: *You have no idea who you are, do you*? Can that still be true?

The Old Salt is shaking his head, apologising with every cell.

'It's okay,' I say. 'Truly.'

We do that clumsy sideways hug that feels a bit embarrassing but is better than nothing when full frontal is too much, or too dangerous. If I had Covid and gave it to him, I'd never forgive myself.

'I'm a fool,' he says again. 'Forget I asked.'

As we go our separate ways, I suspect we both know I won't.

By the time I get home, my head is throbbing. Soon I have a fever, and my body feels like it has been run over by one of the buses that rumble up the hill. I know what this is, so I don't panic. It's a reaction to yesterday's vaccine. I spend the day in pyjamas, shivering and dozing. When I get up to make tea, I notice the other side of the bed is taut, as pristine as though it has just been made. Do I want someone on that side?

No. All I want is sleep.

A COUPLE OF months after Peter died, a friend called.

'Darling, I've seen Pete. Don't think I'm mad, but it was him. He was dancing on the electric wires, like a tightrope walker. He looked so happy.'

She caught me at the wrong moment.

'Well, tell him to get the fuck home. No one's dancing here.'

I don't know what she saw. A fantasy. A ghost. Whatever it was, it enraged me. I'd had no sign or contact, so I made a list on one of his envelopes . . .

THINGS NOT TO SAY TO A WIDOW

- Is it true there were traces of vomit where Peter died?

(I was asked that at his funeral.)

- How are you?
- I don't know how you're still alive. I couldn't go on.

(Ah, that's because you love so much more deeply than I did. Perhaps I should end it now. Would that be an appropriate demonstration of my love?)

- Let yourself cry.

(What makes you think I don't? But why would I cry in front of you?)

- Time is the great healer.

(The shitty thing is I will come to believe this and bleat it to some other widow.)

- You look fantastic, darling. You've lost so much weight.
- God, you look terrible, darling. You've lost so much weight.
- He's in a better place now.
- I understand how you feel.
- He'd want you to find someone else.
- I just know he's watching over you.
- I'm so sorry. My dog died. I so get it.
- It's such a shame you didn't have children.
- It's so lucky you didn't have children.

Worst of all . . .

- Nothing.

The list didn't help.

I'd call his number sometimes, even though I smashed the Nokia within days of his death. Then, as I listened to a voice telling me it wasn't connected, I would remember . . .

Peter, where are you?

Calling and calling.

Where are you, Peter?

Some nights I'd wake, wishing for an apparition, no matter how terrifying.

Then one day I called and a gravelly voice answered; they had reassigned his number, I suppose. I said it was a mistake, hung up and sobbed.

A year after he died, the term *ghosting* appeared in the *Collins English Dictionary*.

> *the act or an instance of ending a romantic relationship by not responding to attempts to communicate by the other party . . .*

I WALK WITH Lisa from downstairs. I meet Marina to swim. I make the daily call to Dad, who has won five dollars on a scratchie. Then I open the Zoom room for our Shakespeare group. We're reading through the complete works, though the century might finish before we do. I use Peter's dog-eared volume, its thin pages annotated in his hand. This month it's *Henry IV, Part 2*. Suffolk gets all the good lines.

> *For where thou art, there is the world itself . . .*
> *. . . And where thou art not, desolation.*

Between acts, I mask up and duck outside to snap a sunset picture from the corner. Thick, ribbed cloud blankets the sky, leaving only an envelope of light in which the city can be seen, a distant jagged outline trying to assert its man-made self between the dark harbour and the puffy ridges overhead.

In the final act, Henry asks: *Can we outrun the heavens?*

I watch a football match from the couch, wearing my Swans sweatshirt and texting other tragics. We use capitals and exclamation marks in lieu of shouting.

At Zoom trivia, we are all stumped by the geography questions. It's like we have no idea where we are anymore. Or I don't. True north has vanished.

What do they say about form following function, Pete? Well, I have no function and I'm in bad form. My gloominess began on the day of the helicopter. I know what it means now, when they swoop the cliffs like falcons. Mostly I shut them out, but that day—was it a week ago? Two?—I couldn't. It buzzed all day.

(I seem to be writing you a letter. Can't help myself.)

Yes, I've kept looking up, and sunsets keep giving. You taught me the French call it *the time between a wolf and a dog*—when the light is so dim you can't make out what's ahead. Well, on any day, there could be a pack of rabid canines in front of me and I wouldn't see them because my eyes are directed skywards at clouds, birds, bats and, occasionally, a plane, always flying west.

Were you hurt when I told the Old Salt that I wasn't sure about having you back? I'm sorry if you were. It's just that sometimes I like this me that is solo-me, and also . . . I've no idea who you would be now. Who would we be?

I walked the labyrinth early today, leaving footprints in frost. It's right at the edge of my five-kilometre radius. When I finished, I sat on my favourite memorial bench.

For Roy, with love. A good man. A good life. 2014.

The same year as you.

Roy and I watched a silver-haired woman creep along the labyrinth's twisting path. Beyond her, the paperbark forest hummed with bats. A heron flew by with a strand of something fibrous in its beak. Myna birds dive-bombed a pigeon. (You'd have been furious.) A gang of galahs shrieked across the blue, as a trail of ants wound around my feet. The creatures went about their business without any thought that a bird might fall mid-flap or a bat might shrivel on a power line. Why can't I?

I stepped tentatively across the green sward so as not to wreak any havoc, but I was stopped by a swoop of swallows. They were winging in circles across the grass, but when they reached me they flew around and around at knee level—chasing insects, I suppose—but their pointed tails and darting movements made me giddy. Around and around they went. Around and around I twirled, trying to see them singly, and to see their patterns together. The joy of it, spinning like a top, surrounded by swallows.

Then, just like that, they were gone, leaving a delirious dancer in their wake, with Will Shakespeare's words in *Richard III* repeating as I slowed.

True hope is swift, Richmond says, *and flies with swallow's wings.*

I saw a murmuration of hope, Pete. And I felt it, in my body. True hope. So very swiftly it came, and my pulse raced, and breath quickened, and my body lifted to the sun, like an offering. Oh, I was all in, Pete. All in life. All for life.

Mind you, hope can leave just as swiftly. Everything contains an opposite, doesn't it? Love holds grief. Laughter becomes tears. With remembering comes forgetting. Some things disappear as others rise. Perhaps that's a kind of forgiveness.

I'm scared, Pete. I do jigsaw puzzles to push back anxieties about people I love. There's reassurance in the click of the pieces and the notion that the world can be nutted out; that something clear can rise from confusion, or something whole from something broken. But of course, once it's done, I pull it apart again.

I try to apply logic. I make lists. They don't help. Did they help you?

I tried tightrope walking! I met this couple in the park: a wiry bloke with dreadlocks and a muscled sprite of a woman. They asked if I'd like a go. I said no, no, I couldn't, but they insisted, so I stepped up. My toes were gripping like a budgie on a swing. The man held my hand—criminal in these Covid times—and I did it. I walked five steps.

So, there has been goodness. The orange fox on the headland, tail high, staring at me with no fear; the beam of light snapping on at the red-and-white lighthouse; the first star; the last bird. Night, dropping slow . . .

I try to get words onto a page. I read and re-read, but my brain won't process because part of it's in the west, where Dad's doing it tough, just as part of it went with you. That sounds like I'm blaming you, Pete, and I don't. It's just that I want this thing done. If I can finish this book, maybe I can be finished with grief.

And yes, I am aware that may be the most stupid sentence I've ever written to you but allow me a bit of superstition. A little leeway, hey?

leeway

I just looked it up. It's on page 816 and you haven't marked it, but you did make a solid line two entries above it, on the *Leeward Islands*.

Did you want to go there, Pete? Why?

Each day, I check the streaming site to see if our peregrines have arrived. I swim. I walk—no surprise there. I'm trying to keep one foot in front of the other under mackerel skies. Best of all is when I spot a whale. It breaks my surface tension.

When I wake, I check the weather in three places. Today was drizzle in Perth, clear in Sydney and cloudy in Melbourne. How is it where you are?

I fret about Dad. He's still so resistant to accepting help. Brett raised the alarm about him living alone, so he has said that he will cop a daily check-in, but I'm frightened for him. I keep the phone close.

I don't sleep, or I sleep then wake, then don't sleep.

I start another jigsaw—a map of Melbourne. Our house is just off the bottom edge. I can't help thinking I'm like a jigsaw with missing pieces. I make myself almost whole, and then I break again. Or lose bits. My writing is a jigsaw too: a fragment here and a fragment there, but I don't seem able to join them together.

I'm tired of the jigsaw metaphor. You'd say I'm overworking it and you'd be right.

We've got online trivia again tonight. I'm readying my questions. I'd like to ask where people go when they die, but it doesn't have a scoreable answer.

This isn't helpful, no matter what that counsellor said. After you died, she told me to write to you, to normalise things. Normalise what? You being ash in a cardboard tube with a leafy forest print on the outside?

Sorry. I'm off song, as Dad would say. Sending love. Wherever you are . . . x

A LONE YACHT dips towards the horizon, like a bird with one wing. I try to describe it to Dad, telling him it's listing, but he's frustrated at not being able to make sense of the word. His breathing catches, and we hang up. Don't worry, Dad. It doesn't matter. It's nothing.

I picture him gasping, straining to hear what the not-important thing was, shut out from conversation by the roar of his lungs.

I walk. I look up. I click. I swim.

The trees in this street, planted close together, keep their dense canopies apart, creating channels of blue like overhead rivers. The phenomenon has a name—*crown shyness*—and is said to be protection against the spread of disease or fungus. Humans are now asked to practise the same behaviour against Covid. I step aside from other walkers, and when a jogger overtakes, I turn away. Will this human 'shyness' help?

Brett says Dad is mostly eating cornflakes. Dad says it's muesli. The Pilgrim can't get solid food down at all. I roast vegetables and simmer lentils, eating for three.

The sky and ocean blur. I have a sense I'm diving upwards and could fall into clouds. Some days I long to let go. Is this the Elegant Backstroker's ascent into unknowing?

Days and days of everydays pass. My seahorses seem to be on strike. Without appointments in my calendar, memory disappears. I go to my Instagram feed, grateful for the journal of daily sunsets.

When I was little, I kept a diary for a while. It had a key and a lock. In it I wrote important things, like having had baked beans for breakfast and a pie for lunch. It went on in this way for a while—Chinese takeaway for special, roast, a letter from an Italian penpal, spaghetti—and then stopped. Lockdown is like that. The lazy same-same of childhood and the anxious same-same of Covid mirror the weary same-same of grief. They flatten out beauty and pain, even euphoria, like a painting in which all the colours are washed with brown. I don't want that to happen. I want to notice shades and shapes, to wake my seahorses, to print the days on myself.

On our thirty-fourth wedding anniversary, I harvest drifts of jasmine from fences. I justify my theft because *jasmine* derives from the Persian for *gift from God*. Shafts of light stream onto the harbour, turning the water into golden syrup—a treat from my childhood diary. The heavens settle back to mauve and finally pink, like the buds of the white flowers I'm holding. Tendrils trail down the front of my Swans jersey as they trailed down my wedding dress.

A pigeon flaps past, its wings beating a message in frantic Morse code. It circles, so near that its movement is like breath on my cheeks. Has it mistaken this place for home? Has it mistaken me for someone else? They say magpies can recognise one hundred faces, but pigeons? It lifts off, up and away, until it's a dot, heading west . . . homing . . .

I watch the last AFL game of the season, texting fellow fanatics, but the Swans lose, and the sky streaks itself with black. Thirty-four years ago I was peeling off my bridal gear and falling onto hotel sheets.

Down by the bay, on the roof of a closed cafe, I spy a peregrine—an ugly, mass-produced plastic replicant, put there to chase away gulls. It's a grotesque parody: the queen of the skies guarding a fish shop, her gormless eyes crossed. The gulls aren't fooled either. They prance about on skinny red legs, their red beaks pecking nonchalantly at the tin roof, red-rimmed eyes twinkling. I stride uphill, fuming at the indignity and wishing my peregrines would hurry up and land on their Melbourne scrape.

At online trivia, I stump everyone. No one knew a baby echidna is called a *puggle*, but no one will forget now. *Puggle, puggle, puggle.*

———

More baked bean and pie days slide by. I post sunsets and bid the stars goodnight, so I haven't stopped looking up. Winter farewells us with a watercolour evening. Birds tweet; wavelets whisper, *shoosh shoosh*; human voices echo across the water. It's a moving image, but so still.

Then comes springy springy spring. Hello, you turbulent thing. On the first day, I walk with three different friends at three different times in three different places within my five kilometres—over 30,000 steps. Everyone is out.

At Parsley Bay, suspended from the white swing bridge, a red heart dangles. A local electrician creates daily light shows there. It's a big, bright heart.

Taking their cue, wattles bloom. There are mare's tail clouds beyond the yellow puffballs. I email a friend: *I had a chat to Dad who sounded really good, so that made me happy.*

Or was it the walking? I could have gone all day, into the night, into tomorrow. I remember that walking euphoria. I only get it when I've gone extra miles, but it's worth it. I am upright. I'm on song.

And then it's Father's Day.

The sky is soft. Dad tells me he 'took a spin' to the shops. They're only 400 metres away, but a drive is a drive, and the car purred. He's tired now, and will sleep. I make tea and return to the jigsaw puzzle. Outside, the sky glows, glazing every leaf of my eucalypt. Not one of them moves.

THE MORNING HEADLINES were a waking nightmare.

BLOATED COD REGURGITATE MICE AMID PLAGUE.

Fish in the Murray River were caught with rodent tails protruding from their mouths.

Scrolling away from that story brought more doom.

SCIENTISTS BREAK DOWN IN TEARS OVER CLIMATE CRISIS.

The lighthouse is waiting, I tell myself. *Keep walking.*

A lighthouse is a kind of keep, like a fortress, and I live equidistant between two. The Macquarie sends out beams like favours bestowed by an empress, her white walls maintained to perfection on a manicured plot of grass, but I'm heading for the Hornby, my court jester with the jaunty weathervane. Striped like a candy cane, her surface is flaky, blistered from constant buffeting by winds and salt.

Wire fencing borders the cliff edge. People attach teddy bears and wreaths, creating shrines so intimate they make me look away. Then, of course, I look back. Sometimes there's a picture. Always smiling. No one photographs a person in despair.

In August 1857, a spanking-new ship called the *Dunbar* was wrecked just below here. One hundred and twenty-one people perished. Bodies and, worse still, body parts washed up around the harbour. Sometimes I imagine the drowned, their skirts billowing and mouths gaping, floating towards me as I swim.

The glittering waters became a crash site. Debris floated into bays and coves. Petticoats and top hats, leather journals and metal trunks, baby bonnets and shoes were strewn around the shores, just like the soft toys and metal shards that splayed across sunflower fields after the crash of Malaysian Airlines flight MH17.

It was shot down two months after Peter died. Sitting on our red sofa wrapped in my blanket, I fixated on the reports, horrified for the families of the 299 people who had died, each now the centre of a shattered community. A gentle writer I knew slightly had been on board with his wife. Their children were interviewed on television, two pale faces lighting up the darkness of the living room.

(How strange, Pete. A *living* room.)

TV stations replayed images, over and over. Cameras tightened on sunflowers, and then the focus would shift to chunks of fuselage, handbags, meal trays, briefcases, water bottles, seats and teddy bears. Always, they showed teddy bears, lopsided and upended, as though this were the ultimate obscenity.

It seemed impossible, unimaginable, unthinkable—reporters used all those words—that the crash could have happened only three months after another airliner, from the same company, had gone missing at sea with 239 people on board. How, reporters asked, could two such disasters occur in so brief a space of time?

Back in 1857, just two months after the sinking of the *Dunbar*, another ship was wrecked off the heads. It was thought navigators had mistaken the location of the Macquarie for the entry point into the harbour. Construction on the red-and-white Hornby began soon after. It's a memorial as well as a working light.

Sunflower seeds from the site of the MH17 crash were germinated in memory of those who died. I scattered Peter's ashes at the base of an oak sapling he planted at our shack, after retrieving an acorn from a tree near Notre-Dame. I gathered friends to tell stories, then poured his gritty remains onto its roots.

Well, not all of them. I had a private ceremony in Melbourne, leaving some of him beneath our birches, and a tiny vial went with his chum to Antarctica. He finally got there. But there's no stone, no plaque, no bench and no words to honour him.

Fresh flowers wither in easterly gales; plastic flowers dull; the coats of teddies fade. These leavings are like the memento mori—translation: remember that you die—in still-life paintings. There, candles and skulls are reminders of mortality. Here, death is beside me, on the fence, while below, waves thrash against sandstone.

Another newspaper reported pink-and-grey galahs falling from the sky. Great piles of them, dead from eating mice that have ingested grain poisoned by humans. Normally, those rose-breasted larrikins live for decades, mating for life and partying on the wing, but these resembled the wilted flowers I see in the cemetery up the hill.

I've become a connoisseur of headstones, lockdown-walking among Celtic crosses and caved-in marble, trying to imagine Muriel and Constance, Winston and Percival. Those names speak of an era before we invented words like *solastalgia: a form of emotional or existential distress caused by environmental change.* I had to look it up online because it's not in your dictionary, Pete. We may need more words for griefs yet to come.

Scientists insist a species will act to further itself, but when will we begin?

Keep walking. Not far now. Blue wrens up ahead. Whales frolicking to the right.

More this year, many more. The pandemic marooned fleets of ships, just as it did the jetliners that are now parked in deserts. Skies and seas quietened as engines stopped, and fronds of seagrass began to grow once more where boats had wiped them out. Researchers heard whales communicating in new, quiet ways where before they'd had to shout, as if they were in a noisy cocktail bar.

Maybe some good can come of all this. Maybe there will be new underwater meadows, and seahorses will dance and make more fry. Maybe . . .

There she is, my red and white beauty. I've found my light.

They used to call that out during technical rehearsals in the theatre. *Find your light.* Warmth caught your forehead, your cheek. Just like this.

I lean into the Hornby, watching fairy wrens courting. Their matchstick legs hop. They twitch and twirl their tails. They chirrup; all cheek and flirt.

Over on North Head, waves pound where the rocks fell, just as they pound below me. In between, the water sparkles, as though some deity has scattered its surface with stars.

I breathe in salt spray and sunshine. I breathe in the light.

FINALLY, FALCONS!

The website is live, and the parent birds are on their concrete scrape, with Melbourne rumbling below. They are done with peregrinations; the time has come to still. The *ding-ding* of a tram counterpoints with the *ek-ek-ek* of a parent bird squatting on precious eggs. It shuffles, then squats again, scanning the darkening sky for its mate.

Skreeeeeeee, he calls when he returns. I can tell it's the male because he's so much smaller, and when he greets his mate I see her speckled female chest. He hops about, inspecting her and the nest and those eggs; inspecting their home.

Oh, happy day.

Two hours pass. I only notice because pain stabs my right shoulder blade. I'm contorted, leaning towards the screen, squinting into black eyes rimmed with fluoro yellow, yet despite

151

the discomfort, I can't leave them. At night, the live stream is grainy and colours leach into greys. Sated after having feasted on a wattlebird, the falcon pair blink at the camera, their hooked beaks opening and closing as though reliving the moment when they ripped apart dinner. I watched, of course. I stared into the glowing rectangle as beaks plunged into feathers and flesh. I observed, just as I did as a child.

So now I have a new routine. (Or is it a ritual?)

On waking, I check the livestream, even before meditation. There they are, blinking in Melbourne's dawn light. The day can proceed. I walk and swim, wondering whether my seahorse is pregnant again; whether they are dancing. I shower at the beach then hurry home to work, but the falcons steal my focus, so I move to the dining table to write by hand. I listen for them, sneaking the occasional peek. I do abandon them for the daily press conference, but invariably I leave it for the sounds of Melbourne and that shrill euphoria-inducing *skreeeee*. Falcons are way more fun than Covid stats.

The parents take turns on the nest. They peer deep into the lens of the webcam, into me, their gaze stern. They've brought the chaos of life back into my home.

The mother is away hunting when an earthquake rocks Melbourne. The father leaves the nest unattended, flying out into the sky, and I hold my breath, wondering if he will return. He does, even before Alanna calls to ask, 'What more can they throw at us? I mean, six lockdowns and now an earthquake!'

Don't tempt the gods, I say, as the falcon father resettles.

I tell Dad about them, but he's more interested in the 'coincidence' that the birds and his car have the same name. He drives an old Ford Falcon, which he services himself with tools he has owned forever. He understands all the workings of the underside of a car bonnet, but streaming technology is impossible to fathom, so instead we discuss his avian visitors. He describes the impudent willie wagtail on the clothesline, and the magpies' heads shifting this way and that, watching him smoke. I want to tell him to stop inhaling that poison. I know a seventy-two-year addiction can't be vanquished overnight, and at his age he should do whatever gives even a jot of pleasure, but my heart won't be rational. Or is the liver the organ of irritability? I don't know, but I'm sure I saw a sparrow's liver go down the gullet of a falcon yesterday.

'We've both got birds for company,' Dad says, before asking how much longer the lockdown might last, and when the state borders could open, and whether I think Covid is going away. 'The world has never seen anything like it before,' he says every time we chat, and I don't know whether it's forgetfulness or amazement that makes him repeat himself, but I wish I could fly across to check.

A friend suggests my brothers install a camera in Dad's unit so we can keep watch. I'm appalled. Even with his body failing, my father would glare harder than the raptor that is eyeballing me now. Dad is proud and private, and the idea of us watching him sleep or ablute, or monitoring food choices, would infuriate him.

I'm as faithful to the falcons as I am to him. When the phone rings, I mute the computer so the caller can't hear the squawks, but my eyes stay fixed on the nest.

I still go out for sunset observations, sometimes with the Pilgrim. Like a newborn peregrine, he can manage only morsels of food, he says. Still, he's determined to brave the cold. He wants to be a person and not a patient, so we talk about books and TV shows, without mentioning the daily radiotherapy countdown that runs in parallel to his lockdown days. In all, by the time he has done, he will have had 107 hits of healing poison. I have to raise my voice to make myself heard from behind my mask, but shouting at him, at his frail frame, makes me feel like a bully. He tells me he is fortunate—that many people are delivering food to him. Soups and custards, soft temptations. People are good, he says.

Like a pigeon, homing, I return to the glowing rectangle. The birds' eyes are pinpricks of white light, but there's majesty in their unblinking gaze. They are free to swing out on updrafts, to dive to earth and rise into sky, to wing to the city's fringes, way past my jigsaw's boundaries. They stare at me, stuck in my room, staring at them. They're busy making baby birds. *What are* you *doing?* they seem to be asking.

I'm keeping watch, I want to tell them. I am turning up for you, you crazy city-dwelling wild things; you, who could choose anywhere, a mountain eyrie or some craggy cliff, have chosen to return to us, to raise your babies in my old home city. You're bringing life to a corner of concrete, and I love you, I want to say, so they can hear me. I love you for your faithfulness, but I am watching over you, just in case. I'm staying the course.

PINK, CIGAR-SHAPED CLOUDS drift above the city. There are more to the east, out to sea. I post a double entry on Instagram and a colleague comments: *Yes, I noticed these too. Lenticular?*

I consult the dictionary. To a soundtrack of Melbourne's night noises—tinkly trams and close-up falcon fluffing—I find the word. It means *shaped like a lentil*. I laugh, but the falcons see nothing amusing in airborne legumes.

Today it's twenty-seven years since Mum died. She smiles from a black-and-white photo on my desk. I'm twenty-five, which makes her forty-six. She's tucked under my arm, her smile twinkly. Mine is more reserved. She was the adult, but sometimes I felt like the grown-up. I have no idea who she would be now.

On arriving at the hospital where she was dying, after a five-hour flight and two-hour drive, I was met by her third husband, who handed me a bag with some nightgowns in it, saying, 'Now you're here, I can go.' That night, I woke from a dream in which he had crashed into a tree and was lying by the road in agony. I felt nothing. Admitting that still makes me ashamed, but maybe it's useful to know I'm capable of such falcon-like disdain.

He never saw Mum alive again.

Nurses came and went. So did Dad. Those two had made their peace long ago. We were all waiting; all going round the bend. And then she went. Now, when I see a parent falcon step off the ledge without a backward glance, I wonder about her. Was death a drop, a plunge, or, like the peregrines, did she lift once she was gone from sight?

I must leave my falcons for work. I'm to interview two other writers. I style my lockdown hair and twist a scarf at my neck, all to the soundtrack of a rainy, twittery Melbourne day. At 4.30 p.m. I switch off the peregrines and set up on Zoom. We'd thought we'd be under warm lights in a room full of readers, but instead we're in our studies, three animated portraits in a virtual gallery, with our audience in living rooms and kitchens, holding cups of tea and glasses of wine.

I get so excited by human company in my study that I gesticulate and disconnect myself, leaving them alone in cyberspace for an agonising two minutes. The panel is called Seismic Shifts. When I finally reconnect, I don't mention the word *eustasy*, though it reverberates for the entire conversation.

Afterwards, I walk into the sunset. Days are lengthening. A late whale, a straggler, puffs and spurts as it races north.

Soon, the falcons will hatch. I speed home to watch them, like a hawk.

The premier gives permission to picnic, so we gather at the deserted cafe by the water. The Pilgrim, gaunt from radiation, is excited to 'break bread', though he can't eat. Other local friends join us, bringing their terrier, Zara, and I ferry food across the park to where we sit, like tourists on a day trip, under the plastic peregrine.

I tell them about the falcon eggs and the kookaburra who visits me at lunchtimes, on my bandwidth of balcony. She's always alone, even though they mate for life. I scratch Zara's ears, remembering Mitzi and Jez. Seagulls hover, relishing this return to normal with its possibility of scraps, while the resident pelican struts among them, snapping his pink bill. Above us, the cross-eyed fake falcon squints down the harbour.

Back at nest-cam, I remember the pilgrimages Peter and I would make to the city high-rise, scanning the skies above backyards and factories. There was always the chance we might glimpse a parent bird on the wing. After all, hope is meant to be a feathered thing.

I start a list . . .

THINGS I WISH PETER COULD KNOW
1. The peregrine falcons are still coming.
2. Notre-Dame Cathedral caught fire, but it's being rebuilt.

3. New words . . . neologisms (he ticked that word): *greenwash, shrinkflation.*

4. There's a teenager called Greta Thunberg who might change the world.

5. I kept his roll of dental floss. I've no idea why. I still have it.

6. I had my wedding and engagement rings remade.

(I removed them the day after he died. They felt like a lie. I was no longer a bride or a wife. I took them to a young woman here in Sydney, and she made a new one, like a cluster of stars. She returned it on the second anniversary of his death and I wear it on my middle finger.)

7. There's Vegemite-flavoured chocolate.

The birds distract me. The list is forgotten.

There are other things, of course, but always, behind them, I hear the *skreeee* of the peregrines. As the Quiet Reading of Books Club convenes on the grass by the harbour for a socially distanced celebratory picnic, part of me is aware that it's drizzling in Melbourne and the parents will be huddling over the eggs.

A writer friend publishes a book of essays, its cover brimful of clouds. At sunset, by the water, the sky mirrors the image in celebration. On my return, I flick through the pages. They smell like possibility. My kookaburra lands, staring deep into me with her enormous soft eyes. Teal feathers pop out from behind the brown on her wings. Her crest is fuzzy, a chocolate-coloured stripe directly above her sharp beak. I breathe in, out, in, out. She stays with me, unafraid, in the gloaming. Can she hear the peregrines?

In the last few days, Dad has sounded increasingly frail. He agreed to be assessed for in-home care, which was great, but he's more and more listless. Maybe it's tuning in to the falcons, but my hearing seems more acute, more creaturely, attuned to his breath. Is this what it is to parent? The promise of someone coming to shower him doesn't allay a gnawing fear that something is wrong and getting more so each day. I worry the winged predator is on approach. My kookaburra keeps staring into me, and I have a sensation that while this moment lasts, everything will be alright. When, eventually, she shakes her head and flies away, I call Dad.

'Did she laugh at you?' he asks.

'No,' I reply. 'We took each other very seriously.'

It's mid-afternoon in Perth. Between breaths, Dad tells me that he's standing at his back door, two 'maggies' on the grass near his feet and a crow on the roof next door. I'm reminded of a picture Marina has been working on—St Francis with birds. I don't tell Dad. He's not religious, and far from saintly, but as he reports his day I hear the magpies warbling, and I'm glad he has company. I also know full well he's standing in that doorway because he's having a smoke.

CHICKS! OH! THERE are chicks.

Well, one, anyway. It's a scrawny dollop of helplessness, naked but for a shadow of down, yet its life force radiates through the camera. I marvel at miniscule stubs that will be wings. Its beak and claws are pink, and its eyes are closed. Its oversized head wobbles, feeble after the effort of entering the world.

This is birth. Well, not precisely. Birth was when its shell cracked open.

Or was it?

What about the moment when the female laid the egg? Once, I saw that happen. The mother had already laid one egg and both parents had left it for periods of time. I was getting anxious when I saw the female return to take up her position on the nest. She sat, staring at the camera, with me staring back, thinking maybe there was only to be one offspring. Then her beak opened and closed, opened and closed, making no sound. She seemed to be in distress, but then she ruffled and settled.

The father flew in and there followed a flurry of pecks and squeaky high-pitched berating, so he left her to it. Alone, she began a curious sort of dance, leaning forward and back, lifting her tail feathers, rocking. The wind ruffled her speckled feathers, adding to the disturbance as she leaned forward, rocked back. Then, she expanded into a mound of feathers and lifted herself, as though she were hitching up a ball gown, about to curtsy, and out dropped an egg, golden in the morning light.

She appeared dazed. She checked it. Yes, it was there. She stood, letting her 'skirts' rustle in the breeze, and then the moment that made me want to applaud: she shimmied her stripy feathers back into place and swung her falcon hips, for all the world like she was damn proud of herself, before settling back down onto the two glowing eggs.

Was that birth? If not, it was something like it. I've seen death in various guises, but that was wonderment. Not *wonder*. The dictionary says *wonderment* contains awe. That moment did. And so does this one.

The chick shudders. I lean in to meet its huge blind eyes, glad it can't yet see the expanse beyond its nest—the horizon, the offing, the nearby skyscrapers and the yawning drop. If it looked down, its tiny heart might stop.

I leave it but swim fast, rushing back to witness the arrival of the next ball of newness. I dash out again before dark, wanting to see how the Pilgrim is faring; like the chicks, he strains at the sky, hungry for life despite radiation and the bite of surgery scars. The sunset ritual must be kept, because constancy has given me the falcon babies. They're perfect—four tufted infants that will become gods of the firmament. Bow down to the sky in which they'll fly. Bow to the moon, rising like a lucky penny as the sun sets.

Do seahorses and falcons feel hope? Oh, I hope so. I hope for them as I click, click, click. Overhead, moody blues erupt from egg-gold layers and god-light. Then a funnel of thunderous thick grey appears, as though the firmament is being bisected by the wing of a mammoth raptor, spreading from the sea to the city. We *peregrinos* gaze up until our necks hurt, then catch each other's eyes and shake our heads. Why try to speak in the face of majesty? If the chicks could see this, they would be silent, too.

I find a website to learn about their struggle to be born, which began almost three days ago. First, they must eat all the yolk that's left to strengthen themselves for what lies ahead. Then they position themselves for most leverage, beak protruding from between body and winglet. They make sounds to alert Mum and Dad to their arrival. Then—and this makes me shiver— they take their first breath, still inside the shell. There's an air bag at one end, and the chick must break this to inhale. Air floods into tiny lungs for the first time. What, oh what, must that inflation feel like?

Then it begins to pip. The chicks have a special egg tooth for this purpose, as well as a ridge of muscle down the back of the neck to assist with the breaking of the shell. The process is called *pipping*.

The chick makes a hole. Then a seam. During all this work, it must rest often. Rest is everything. Restore. Gather. Get ready for the final push when the wee feet are engaged to break through the shell and into the day.

How do they know to do all this? The word *instinct* is only two syllables.

The chick is wet when it arrives. A lump of exhausted, breathing sinew and blood and fluff, it has pipped its way into life and is now a *hatchling*.

I lean back from the screen, dumbstruck with admiration for the four sibling splodges. On the thirty-fifth floor, a feathered miracle has occurred. Why is there not singing in the streets? Only the thrum of trains and trams and the occasional warning toot breaks the night silence. I keep watch, as proud as if they were my own.

Daylight saving begins. The time difference between me and Dad extends to three hours. I must now wait until at least noon before I call to report on the babies. I spend more and more time with them. I spend more and more time with clouds. I've stopped feeling pointless. I've stopped lying awake with a thumping heart; stopped fretting about being unable to make work or find work; even stopped feeling guilty that I can't cross state lines to see Dad. There are chicks, and they hold me in my state of wonderment.

On the first day of October, more than three months after we locked down, the state premier resigns. We'd trusted her as she kept our borders open and fed us daily information. No matter the political persuasion, we mostly accepted her decisions, because she seemed to listen to science and the chief medical officer. She leaves because of allegations of corruption. Oh, I say. Oh.

The falcons aren't bothered, and the skies stay clear. The pelican at the wharf still struts regally past the row of dinghies, and the whale highway is busy with breaching babies. I keep turning up to the peregrines, as the new premier, a skinny Conservative with a French-sounding name, tells us we're to exit lockdown earlier than anticipated. Next Monday, he says. It feels rushed. Premature. I don't want to flee the nest, though I long to fly.

Then Dad tells me he fell. He was getting the shopping bags from the back seat of the Falcon, and he toppled. It wasn't bad, honey, he says. It was like a tree listing to one side. It will be fine, sweetheart. But I picture his bony frame hitting concrete and bags tumbling around him, and the cracking, and his unstoppable bleeding, and the myriad bruises that will ensue, and I curse his state premier who keeps borders closed, even as I try to maintain calm and read Dad's voice to see whether or not he really is okay, because it actually happened two days ago and he didn't tell me because he knew I would worry, and of course I will worry; and I ask what he is doing and he says he is pouring a wine and will have a cigarette, and I ask if he needs to see the doctor, and he says no, he doesn't want to, he just wants to be quiet and he will be fine, darling, I will be fine, don't you worry. I'm just resting, he says. Rest is the thing. I ask about food, and he promises he's eating, but he's a bit sick of the delivered meals and might try to cook something but don't worry, honey, it's all fine. He hangs up to have his 'ciggie and vino'.

I pace my flat. I pace the shore. I want to cry but won't. Hold it in. Hold it in.

The hatchlings are hungry. Mouths agape, they strain and topple, but never seem perturbed, even near the edge. If they fell, they'd plummet thirty-five storeys onto city pavement, but their focus is only here and now. Food. Sleep. Sunshine.

Three years ago, I fell. My head smashed onto concrete, my face scraped along loose gravel, my wrists took my full bodyweight and my kneecaps banged down, thudding and skidding. I wailed like a broken animal.

Thankfully, the weather eyes of the morning swimmers were on me. Ambulances arrived—two of them—checking and rechecking for concussion or brain damage. Marina followed. I was monitored and comforted, then taken home and nursed by her. But for days afterwards, waking or sleeping, I'd recall my head plunging towards the path.

I knew how fragile the brain was. Peter's death had shown me that one treacherous vessel was all it took, and now it was as though the two seahorses in my head had got stuck, dancing in the same groove over and over. I fell, and fell again, every time I closed my eyes. Marina said to rest, but my hands flailed. Pavement kept roaring up to meet me. Being alive, my seahorses insisted, was merely the difference between strolling and tripping. I shook and shivered, trying not to see the ground rushing towards my forehead.

That quivery panic was familiar from the months after Peter's death. Someone called it hypervigilance, but I experienced it as an acute awareness that catastrophe was upon all of us, constantly; that the reality we take for granted—a continuum of daily ordinariness, broken by little triumphs or setbacks—is a furphy, invented to shore us up against the hard-as-concrete truth that everything is precarious and all time is borrowed. I'd worked so hard—learning to swim and telling myself that reinvention and happiness were possible—but with the fall, I regressed to those early days of grief.

I'd also regressed into a state of disconnection from my body. I didn't want this 'thing' that could break and bleed. Falling was a reminder that I was just flimsy flesh and sinew, as were all the people I loved. If I, who held up planes, could fall, so could they.

So could everyone, said the grief counsellor, six months after Peter died. We all fall, she told me, as we sat in her inner-city office with its bare walls, the branches of a plane tree lashing at the arched window. We fall ill and we fall out, she said. We fall short. Everyone does. We can fall through cracks. And eventually we fall away, like leaves from deciduous trees.

I nodded, feigning understanding, my eyes on the tree. Her words felt right and good—poetic, even—and surely if I listened hard I would understand the lesson she wanted me to take from them, but I was too busy looking for a nest, which had been a constant through our sessions and now was gone. In hindsight, maybe she was asking me to allow acceptance.

There are times when it comes and my old sunny security returns, but maybe that's a kind of wilful forgetting. After all, things are measurably worse than when he died. Every species is threatened by the climate crisis, wars erupt, refugee camps overflow, and greed is as good as it ever was. Other friends have died suddenly: one fell down a flight of stairs; one dropped while doing online aerobics; another took a nap and never woke.

As I walk with the Pilgrim under a vermilion sky, he says forgetting is a kind of protection. We need memory banks, he maintains, but we also need space for deposits. If we filled every corner, there might be too much focus on what we've lost; too much regret and nostalgia; too much mourning. That doesn't stop me from watching his feet as we approach a bit of wonky pavement.

My brother Brett says grieving is like walking. His adored wife died of an aneurysm four years before Peter. You'll get stronger, Brett tells me. You'll go longer, and gain confidence. But remember—you can be cruising along when, *bang*, you'll fall. And, he says, you'll fall further each time, because you've climbed higher towards acceptance in the interim.

Romance literature insists we *fall* in love, and perhaps that does describe the tumult of the beginning days. When Peter and I went to pledge our troths, we learned the word derives from *truth*, which made us doubly serious about getting our lines right. We didn't invoke forever. We changed one vowel in our vows, promising to stay together '*as long as we both shall love*'. We thought we were so clever, but we forgot that love could outlive life.

Now, I walk through the final days of lockdown, clicking photos, returning to the falcons, trying to write, talking to Dad. I pace and pace, taking care not to trip. Not now, not at the last gasp. I stride along the shore, the headland, the clifftops. I march around the park and stroll through the cemetery, greeting stone angels, noting stories of drownings and infant deaths and speaking aloud forgotten names. Lockdown is ending, Winnie. We've nearly made it, Walter. Only a few days now, Hilda.

I climb steep back lanes, where star jasmine tumbles over broken fences in pungent clouds. I tackle 'Heartbreak Hill' and reward myself with the lighthouse circuit. I stand under the Hornby, watching her beams reach into the evening glow.

I cover miles and miles, and on 10 October I stop to take a breath, realising that suddenly I'm here, at the finish, and I look up and click, and post a picture that is all blues, every shade. I note beneath the image that *the sky never let me down*.

I remind Dad it's our last locked-down day, and that soon, surely, his premier will open that border and I will be winging over to see him. It's ten months since I visited, and I'm frightened by how wan he sounds. My voice wobbles as I tell him I love him. He has no breath, so I hang up and return to the falcons, staring at the screen, just as I stared down that road, willing Dad to turn the corner, the scent of lavender wafting around me. I watch my nestlings but can't shake the sense that something is horribly wrong, so when my brother Justin calls I'm awake, waiting.

Dad has had a collapse. Justin puts him back to bed because he doesn't want hospital. I speak to him to see if he'll change his mind, but he's adamant: no fuss. Justin is, as ever, patient and wry. He has been able to get Dad to eat some cheese and biscuits, but it's clear all he wants is bed. He has been like this since the fall: too tired to bother; no delight, no relish.

Gratitude, acceptance, stoicism—none of those demand physical exertion. Delight, though, requires breath, and Dad is beyond it. Apparently, he has been surviving on a handful of muesli, a glass of wine and a cigarette. Not exactly a Shakespeare sonnet.

I email the others. We agree we'll need to take action tomorrow, but for now, we must wait. He is not a child, and his wishes are clear. I spend the final night of lockdown keeping vigil. There's rarely a movement in the nest, just a ring of fuzz underneath the female falcon, but I stay, staring, blinking, watching. I will not desert my post.

In the pre-dawn hour, as I pray to any god that will listen to open up that bloody border into WA, one of my seahorses squirms, and I remember that when I was little, Dad always called me 'Chick'.

Still life with flowers

IN A WHITE ceramic bowl lay a ring—silver, edged with gold. A watch nestled alongside, its second hand quivering with each tick. Curled under it was a band made of leather entwined with silver.

To the right of the bowl, two photographs. The first was unframed, showing a hand against the pages of a dictionary. On the third finger was the silver and gold ring. The second, framed in dark wood, was a portrait of a man gazing directly into the camera. Beside it, sprays of white phalaenopsis orchids rose from a vase, their flowers ghost-moths, hovering above a candle's flame.

This was a still life of my own making, but I couldn't inter-pret, or intuit, its meaning. My fingers went to the paper in the pocket of my grey dress—his envelope list. Still there. Still tangible. Still . . .

Before emails and texts, I could recognise the handwriting of every person I loved. Seeing Peter's on that list of repairs had been as potent as hearing his voice.

Well, no. That would have meant he was alive, and handwriting couldn't work that magic, but the envelope was the one thing I'd picked up from beside our bed. I didn't know it then, but eventually I would use his list to prepare the house for sale. It guided me, which was just as well, because I was never bothered by squeaky floors or laundry cupboards that stuck.

Sometimes, I forget about the list, and when I remember, I rush to locate it. It isn't sacred. It's just a catalogue of repairs, a practical guide to a future that might have been, that led me to a future I hadn't imagined. If his list has any sanctity, it's in the intentions it carried and the guidance it gave. It was as though he wrote it for me; a lifeline.

That first chilly Melbourne morning, clutching it, I turned away from our bed, intending to put as much distance as possible between me and the pink-stained sheets. At the doorway, though, I was stopped by a familiar. There, on the walnut tallboy that had belonged to his eccentric aunt, was his favourite item of clothing: the dusky-blue 'survival shirt', with its pockets for pens or snacks or the hated Nokia. He'd been wearing it when I last saw him.

'Go quickly so you can come back quickly.'

Peter rarely articulated emotions but, like Dad, he understood practical love. He washed my car until it gleamed and blacked the tyres with special goop. He brought home irises with the broccoli. He flew across the country to be with Alanna and me at Mum's deathbed.

Many years later, I sat with him as his mother drifted into not-knowing. I was there when she batted her eyelashes at him, saying, 'Oh, doctor, what a lovely head of hair you have.' We laughed then, but I couldn't stop his sobbing when he had to admit her to an aged-care facility—we never used the word 'home' because it wasn't that, despite its plush sofas. He turned up for her, a constant, as she faded and died.

We held each other as our dog was put to sleep—an accurate euphemism for what happened when the vet arrived that scorching afternoon with the needle of green liquid. We stroked his fifteen-year-old corpse and Peter buried him with a favourite squeaky toy and a single white lily. We planted bulbs and annuals above him.

All those tender mercies I'd seen Pete perform; yet, as I stood on the threshold of our bedroom, I knew I wouldn't be able to do any of them for him. He was in a cold metal tube, in a place with a temperature like Antarctica's.

The shirt lay there, lifeless. Last time I'd seen it, it had wrapped around my uncertain frame as planes crisscrossed overhead. Its sleeve had waved me goodbye. I could smell it, smell him, as though he were still inside it: laundry soap, sweat, wood smoke, citrus.

Peter.

I wanted to touch it but didn't dare. I knew the feel of it with his body inside it, and now it was just a rag.

Four days after his death, during the interminable wait for the coroner to release his freezing body, Alanna said I should go through his clothing.

'If you don't do it now, you never will,' she insisted. 'And it will be easier with me to help.'

Everything was easier with Alanna. We worked from pre-dawn till deep dark, keeping, binning, gifting to friends and donating to the op shop up the road, where many items had been bought. One afternoon, I stood at the front gate, watching her lug a suitcase past picket fences to the volunteer ladies who'd always kept aside 'special' garments for Peter. When she returned, her eyes were red and swollen, but she just shook her head and we gravitated to the kettle.

She was there when I had to choose an outfit for him to wear to his own funeral. I didn't pick the survival shirt; it was too informal, I told Alanna, as though somewhere there was a dress code for what to wear to your cremation.

I selected a shirt he'd bought in Paris on that long-ago anniversary holiday. It was navy with a fine white spot; the cuffs and collar white with a navy spot. He had darned it, as he did with many favourites. We took it to the funeral director, along with plain black trousers and shoes, black underpants, and a pair of thick socks to keep his toes warm.

Peter was tall, with full lips and soft eyes. I thought him beautiful, but I couldn't bear to see him when the funeral director offered. I knew that the coroner had peered inside his skull, and I was not brave enough to look into his lifeless eyes, knowing someone had examined that questing mind. Or brain. Or psyche.

(Why don't I know the right word, Pete?)

Like so many choices I made then, I took a step in a direction and committed to it, but maybe to have held his icy hand, stroked his thick hair, rubbed his cold feet—maybe that might have made me understand in my bones that he was gone, because I didn't—or wouldn't—for the longest time. Even now, it's possible to imagine him on tour, in another state, or Japan or London, where work had taken him before. Away, not gone.

Except it isn't possible. Not really. When he was touring, I knew where he was and could align myself to him. There was no fear because he was still my compass point. Now, the needle spins and I can't get my bearings.

Still, it's easier to picture him 'elsewhere' than to imagine him as dust, like the grains that blew onto my bare legs when I scattered his ashes at the shack, running from them, the wind flinging specks of him at me as I fled downhill.

But that came later . . .

In the lead-up to the funeral, as we waited for the coroner to release his body, Alanna listened to me fret over every decision. She made lists—Peter would have approved. She poured tea. She arranged a venue for the wake and coordinated friends. She searched for photographs to make a perfectly timed montage to the song 'Nature Boy'.

Once, she found me sitting at the dining table, typing. 'Oh that's the best thing, my sis,' she said.

'What?'

'You typing. It's the first time you've looked normal.'

I was writing his eulogy.

Not long after the funeral and wake, and after Alanna had flown home to Perth, where she was living then, I opened the doors of Peter's empty wardrobe to be walloped by his scent. There he was, as though alive. I closed and opened the doors, breathing him in. It was like a kind of enchantment—the way those doors returned him to me. If scent is molecules, maybe I was literally taking him into my body.

More than once—no need to admit how often—I huddled inside with the doors closed. Scrunched there, as small as I could be, I'd imagine the door creaking open to reveal Narnia, the world C.S. Lewis dreamed, which had been so vivid to me in childhood. I could almost see the frozen land, like an Antarctica populated with talking mice, where things would always be put right by Aslan, the great lion-god who could restore spring. I never saw Peter, though. No magic and no transports.

The empty wardrobe took me nowhere, but at least it reduced the world to a size I could manage.

Months later, I would find his blue survival shirt in the bag where I'd stashed it. I would pull it out and inhale, and I would wail. Then I'd castigate myself for behaving like a character in a B-grade movie and shove it back into the bag. The push-pull of feeling and shutting down, releasing and holding, became a familiar rhythm of those days.

That first morning after his death, though, I was still trying to force truth in through my unwilling pores.

Dead. He is dead. Look. See.

On the tallboy, beside his survival shirt, was a fading photo from our first summer together, twenty-seven years, five months and thirteen days earlier.

Lying in front of it was his wedding ring. I couldn't bear to think of them yanking it over his knuckle, even as another part of me knew he would have been dead, feeling nothing. Beside it lay his watch, a wedding gift from me, first worn, like the ring, twenty-six years, eight months and twenty days earlier.

Next to them was a leather wristband, bought to celebrate our twenty-fifth wedding anniversary, one year, eight months and twenty days earlier.

I grabbed it, along with the ring and watch. In the kitchen, I chose a bowl to hold them, placing it on a rickety wooden side table. In my study I found two framed photos. The smaller one was taken for a friend's birthday. The idea was that we'd all have our hands photographed doing something typical, and the collection would be bound into a book. Peter's hand was snapped on a page of his previous dictionary, his wedding ring shiny against his pale Irish skin, and his little finger pointing to the word he'd chosen.

enthusiast

I'd always assumed I knew its meaning, but when I checked, I learned it can also mean *a self-deluded person*. Peter smiled straight at me from the larger framed photo. He had often called me an enthusiast.

Then—a knock at the door. Maybe an error? Maybe—maybe . . .

A man in a khaki shirt held a box of white flowers.

'Ailsa?'

We gawped at each other. I shook my head.

'Flowers for Ailsa,' he said, holding out the quivering blooms. He was scared, this big sturdy bloke. Normally, he was met with gratitude, but clearly this was not normal. He pushed the arrangement into my unwilling hands and rushed away down the brick path, where the bell on the gate clanged, over and over, as he tried to get the latch to close behind him. What had he seen that frightened him?

So began the ritual of the flowers.

That first box of orchids heralded a torrent of tenderness in floral form: white magnolias and maroon peonies; crimson lilies, blue hydrangeas and roses—pink and white, red and yellow;

carnations, chrysanthemums and hyacinths; gum blossoms and proteas, daffodils and jonquils; poppies and snapping dragons and birds of paradise; tight tuberoses and frothy tulips.

They came for weeks, and each icy morning, before sunrise, I'd move from vase to vase, snipping, trimming and rearranging, creating new still lifes. Perhaps those freesias would look better behind his binoculars? Spiky strelitzias might contrast with the wooden bowl he'd bought in Tasmania. I turned up to the flowers religiously: removing leaves and shortening stems, adding sugar to water and deadheading.

Peter had put two lines beside *deadhead* on page 366 of his dictionary.

1. *a faded flower-head*
2. *a passenger or member of an audience who has made use of a free ticket*
3. *a useless or unenterprising person*

I didn't linger over which meaning had compelled him.

I cared for the flowers because I could no longer care for Peter. More than having someone to look out for me, I missed someone who was mine to tend. Then, when the flowers died, I had to let them go. They showed me, better than any coroner or doctor, that I couldn't keep anything alive beyond its time. Dropped in the bin, rank with decay, they were a reminder that even beauty ends. In fact, they insisted, it's more precious *because* it ends.

But that first morning, I placed the white box on the wooden table and stepped back, letting my gaze range over the still life. What had I made? It was not the usual arrangement of objects juxtaposed with each other to create a narrative. No. This was something else. It was a shrine.

I hated myself in that nanosecond of comprehension. I hated the treacherous corner of my mind that had allowed reality to step in. Now, there was no going back.

IT's MORNING ONE of post-lockdown life, and I'm waiting for news from Perth. Marina arrives, bringing flannel flowers. She's the first human visitor to my flat in 107 days. I mute the falcons, and we talk. I'm struck by the vividness of her black eyes and curls. Her movements seem choreographed as she tucks a leg under her body. All this life—the specificity and uniqueness of her. Her voice bounces off walls and windows, distracting me from the incessant bleating of the new baby magpies in the eucalypt. Unlike the falcons, they can't be silenced.

I stand the flannels in a tall vase that was a gift from Peter, placing them, just so, next to a wooden carving of the word *HOPE*. I'm conscious of composition in Marina's presence. They say there's a language of flowers, and I wonder what these signify, but there's no time to check. My friend is here, in my home, sipping tea, and I feel myself being brought to life like a character that has been dozing for 100 years.

Till human voices wake us . . .

Marina describes her latest still life. I slip between times and places, then and now rising and falling.

Till human voices wake us . . .

Peter was in a film of that title. He played a father who was unable to express affection to his son.

Marina asks about Dad. I tell her Brett should be almost with him by now.

The past swirls. Peter's face on a big screen. I try to stay present. Today is for Dad and my visiting friend. It's for celebration. It's Freedom Day.

Marina leans forward, her hand reaching to accept a biscuit, and my seahorses dance, retrieving a memory. She'd asked me to pose for a picture because she couldn't quite get the shape of a body.

'Just sit on that bench,' she'd said. 'Now bend your arm at ninety degrees. Lean your torso forward. Stop. That's it.'

I sat, observing my hand, palm up. The lines, the moles, the scars. Then I saw the whole arm. What was it doing, suspended out there in mid-air?

'Am I begging?'

Marina looked up, blinked, refocused. 'No,' she said. 'You're offering seed to birds.'

I was startled, realising the body doesn't differentiate between asking for help and making an offer; between giving and receiving. I think about my father, and how stubbornness and grace battle within him—independence is vital, yet he tries to accept our opinions and help.

Now, Marina nibbles at shortbread, sips peppermint tea, and we talk of the progress of that picture, of her mother and sister, her upcoming exhibition and the harbour's warming temperature. Her voice wakes my sleeping home.

After she leaves, I return to the falcons. They squawk, as though in dialogue with the baby magpies, and flap their wings, rehearsing flight. Their fluff is being replaced with feathers and they're like a pack of thuggish little gang members as they wait to rip into the third, fourth, fifth delivery of prey from their overworked parents. Outside my window, parenting magpies make a similar to-and-fro feeding relay. The flannel flowers nod their approval.

Eventually, there's a ping on my phone—a message from Brett. Dad will be taken to hospital in an ambulance. A chick lifts its scrawny neck and shrieks. *Bring food! Bring food!* it demands in an ear-splitting pitch, its beak widening to reveal the pink interior of its mouth. I pray that today Dad will let nourishment slide down, maybe even enjoy it.

I make more tea and eat too many biscuits as I wait, watching the nestlings. The correct term is *eyas: an unfledged bird, usually a hawk*. One *eyas* lies flat, a sated furball on a clump of bones and droppings. Its black bead-eyes are fixed on me. It has already perfected its death stare and can spot weakness. From the eucalypt, the magpie babies sound vulnerable.

On the other side of the continent, Dad will be going through the hospital admissions process. His weight has slipped from fifty-eight kilograms three months ago to fifty-four three weeks ago to forty-nine this week. He is chalky bird-bones and thin, papery skin, like a peregrine chick without feathers. I want to screech at the doctor-gods. *Help Dad! Help Dad!*

A train whistle blares. The chicks' feathers shimmer, a collective ruffle in response to the sound. Their mouths open and close, appetites insatiable. Dad's is nonexistent. The chicks are raucous, their hearts formidable, while Dad's is precarious because the pig valve that was inserted into it fifteen years ago is dying. Fifteen years multiplied by twelve months by seven days by twenty-four hours by sixty minutes by sixty seconds . . .

A lot of work for a porker.

The beady-eyed chick glares at me. *What's your problem, lady?* A bigger sibling lifts its head to catch some winter sun. Another stretches a winglet, and the smallest shifts from foot to foot on the outer before finding a space to nestle.

Do they know they are on the edge of an abyss?

———

News from Perth. Brett says Dad seemed relieved when the ambulance was called. He put up no resistance but simply got out of bed, saying it was probably a good idea, son.

Beady opens its beak wide like a drowning fish on sand. A sibling pushes a claw out from the huddle then snuggles back under its parent. These babies will reach maturity under the gaze of thousands of us, all over the world. There are grey metal louvres to the left, bits of broken shell on the ledge beside them, some white streaks of shit, and the picked-over bones and feathers of their home delivery. The chicks are unconcerned about aesthetics. They jostle then sleep. The early days of living are like the fading of life, small and dozy.

An email arrives from Brett. Its subject line is *Good Spirits*. There are two photos. In one, Dad is on a gurney, held in place with red and black straps, ready to roll. He grins and gives a thumbs-up sign. In the second, he's in his garage with the ambulance in the background. One skeletal hand clutches a packet while the other holds a cigarette near his grinning face. He looks as happy as the proverbial pig, puffing while paramedics wait. A last gasp.

The chicks screech. Their hunger makes them furies. Beady begins a piercing wail. I make tea, but hurry back to them. I must not leave my station.

A parent peregrine appears, yellow markings like warnings around its eyes. It prods the pile of offspring then settles, before fixing its gaze on me. This is what care looks like, it says. This is what it is to be responsible. To be here, day in, day out, to turn up to those who are yours.

The other adult brings a fantail from down in the square. It's no wonder fighter jets have been named after peregrines. They set upon the prey, ripping into it as their belligerent babies scream for flesh, blood, gizzards. I munch Vegemite toast.

Three currawongs, their black plumage glinting, land on my balcony railing. They're a funereal chorus line. *Curra, curra, curra*, they call, before lifting their tail feathers to dump identical grainy squirts onto the balcony tiles and lifting off in flapping unison. I'm appalled.

Dense liquid pools, viscous and dark, like the bruises on Dad's legs. Yesterday, he reported he was 'fair to muddling'.

'Well, more muddling than fair, really, darling,' he wheezed.

He may be in a ward by now. With a little of his luck, he will be sleeping, safe under the eyes of a medical team, just as the peregrines doze under mine.

A WEEK ON, and Dad's still in the geriatric ward. Desperate for a cigarette, his addiction makes him fractious, then strategic. He wants to go home to tend his roses and 'a few other things', but when pushed, he admits it would really be a chance to smoke.

When news finally comes, it's bad. The fall tipped him over an edge, and he will not be able to live alone anymore. Like the seahorse, he must be relocated. At ninety-one, he will need to adapt.

The good news is that Melburnians are to be freed in three days. My sisters rejoice. Over the course of twenty months, they will have endured 250 days of lockdown.

The falcon siblings now have dark feathers on their tails and wings; glossy striations replace billowy down. They tussle when a parent brings kill, and rarely pile together to sleep anymore. They are individuating. One is noticeably larger, always the first to any food. Was it born more aggressive, or did it develop this dominance? Chicken or egg? It will mature into a sleek grey dart; a missile.

We human siblings are a team with a mission. Brett liaises with social workers and hospital staff while Justin manages mail redirections, fridge clearing and powers of attorney. From Melbourne, Amanda consults with Dad's medical team, and Alanna, who is not Dad's daughter, offers support and encouragement. I am charged with finding respite care and then, reluctantly, a permanent placement. A home. I wince every time I say the word.

Dad rarely complains, despite it being his worst nightmare, and even admits to feeling a bit safer in hospital. I do, too. I sleep through nights, knowing there are nurses nearby. I meditate at 6 a.m., then walk, thieving gardenias wherever I may, before swimming up a storm. I breakfast while researching the aged-care system in the west. I try for an hour of my own work until 11 a.m., when I click over to Perth time, where it's 8 a.m., and begin phone calls and follow-up emails. With the fruity scent of stolen flowers wafting about, I cross-reference staff turnover, distance from Justin's house, ratios of carers to residents, presence of a registered nurse, how funding is arranged—and, of course, the possibility of Dad being able to smoke on the grounds. There is none. Forget it, they all say.

How will we tell him?

That's for later. Keep going.

I inquire about food preparation, recreational spaces, support workers and activities. I check online reviews and ask for references from friends and friends of friends. I call in favours and try to wheedle into good books. I'm doing okay, but then I blow it when a woman from one of my preferred places returns my call and tells me her surname. It's Death.

'Death?' I snort. Actually, I laugh. A lot. I corpse.

Silence.

'I'm sorry,' I splutter. 'It was a shock. You know . . . my father is so weak and it's my biggest fear . . .'

My voice tails off. A crow *aaaarks* somewhere nearby. I apologise again, and eventually she says it's not the first time and we move on, but the eyes of the falcons are trained on me with that look that says I am weak and I must die.

Days speed. Time flies at peregrine pace. Jacarandas flower, then carpet the streets purple. The Melbourne chicks fatten, flap and fight as magpie offspring wheeze incessantly in my euca-lypt. Parent birds bring takeaway in both cities, their hatchlings in stereo, as my fingers click-clack and I repeat my queries to another welcome manager.

After a fortnight, Dad moves from hospital into respite care, and immediately finds a way to steer his new wheelie-walker through locked doors and past reception to sit under a tree and enjoy a cigarette or ten. He says he's back on song. He takes himself out for a haircut and I panic. He can't fathom why. He's losing weight again, but the staff assure us he's doing well. He's so charming, they say. Dad has few possessions but is rich in manners and curiosity, and they serve as passports.

So, he 'takes the sun' and puffs, chuffed whenever Judy visits and he has a partner in crime. I hunt for permanent options, scanning like a parent bird for opportunities. My brothers inspect those I deem possible, while the peregrines bicker and strengthen at the edge of their ledge, watching their parents swoop and skim past, showing them how flying is done. I tender applications, while the magpies make tentative flights to Lisa's balcony railing. We are advised of available dates and our choices narrow as the peregrines flap adolescent wings, building strength before they take that thirty-five-storey leap.

Dad is taken for tests: suspected cancer in his throat and the dicky valve in his heart; mysteries in his blood and tissue-thin lungs. There might be something in the pancreas, they say, but then, no, it's nothing, Amanda reports. He's winding down while the peregrines are winding up, their eyes on the sky. I worry they will fall. I worry Dad will falter.

One night he wakes to find an old woman beside his bed, holding his hand.

'What did you do?' I ask. 'Were you freaked out?'

'No,' he says. 'I told her it was nice of her to visit but maybe she should go back to her room and we could see each other in the morning. She was just lonely, darling.' His matter-of-fact understanding of the woman's plight tells me something I don't want to hear.

I keep up my remote hunt, and in late October my brothers take Dad to visit a place I think has prospects. It's the first he has sighted, and he says it will be the one. He doesn't need to compare.

'It's fine, sweetheart. Just fine.'

Close to Justin, it's small and humble, but the staff are welcoming and there's an inner courtyard garden planted with callistemons and roses, and a leafy street for smoking. One woman tells him she has lived there for twenty years.

He is waitlisted.

To all this upheaval, he says yes. We know there is disappointment; even, at times, despair. It's not what anyone wanted, but we take our lead from him.

'You have to accept, at my age, sweetheart,' he says. 'I'm luckier than lots of people.'

Perhaps he's remembering my stepmother and Peter and Brett's wife. Me, I wonder if sudden death really might be kinder, as people have insisted to me over the years; but I'm sure there's error in conflating a diminishing life with death. Dad is still here. He's in the world, even if he's shrinking. He's living, not dying.

I have a photo of him at twelve months. The 'lucky man' began as a wide-eyed cherub, with snowy hair and a sweet, open face. Are we humans like trees, with our first inner ring defining who we are? Or did Dad learn his acceptance over time, as his outer rings were attacked by losses? Dad's great triumph is the story he tells about himself. Perhaps 'lucky' is his inner ring.

One of the peregrine chicks is noticeably smaller than the others. They jostle it about, and when food arrives, they show no compassion. It must wait for leftovers.

runt

I find four definitions.

1. *a small pig, esp. the smallest in a litter*
2. *a weakling; an undersized person*
3. *a large domestic pigeon*
4. *a small ox or cow, esp. of various Scottish Highland or Welsh breeds*

There's also an adjective that was coined in the sixteenth century: *runty.*

Runty waits as the parents bring pigeons from city streets and his stronger siblings rip into them. He waits as they extend their wings and stretch their claws. He waits, staring across the Melbourne skyline, the Arts Centre spire, the casino, the office buildings, all full of people unaware they're being watched. He waits, blinking in the direction of the Botanic Gardens and all those ancient trees. He waits. As we do.

AND IT'S NOVEMBER. After the crawl of lockdown, I'm dizzy with the whirl of time while simultaneously impatient that Dad still shares a ward and has no privacy.

'Don't worry, darling; I went to boarding school for a while.'

'That was nearly eighty years ago.'

'Some things you never forget, honey!' He laughs. I do, too.

Undersized, but no weakling, he waits for the 'vacancy' we all understand is doublespeak for a death.

Runty stands apart from the others, tucking in tight against the wall of the building, folding in on himself while his siblings stand at the edge, testing their now-powerful wings, simulating flight. This instinct—is it that, or have they learned from watching their parents?—will not be denied. They beat at the air, their wings wider each day, the flapping increasingly intense, but how will they know when it's time to step off the edge?

Who will tell them it's safe? What if they launch, only to drop hundreds of metres?

Each morning, as I lift off from the sand to begin my swim, I think of them.

Occasionally, Runty inches forward, but mostly he seems to have decided to be an audience for his siblings. Has he learned acceptance? Is this his nature, or is he unwell? The others have golden feathers on their chests and their legs are long. Runty pecks at their leftovers.

Dad masters the mobile phone Justin buys—not bad at ninety-one—though he curses it in much the same way I cursed Peter's Nokia. Dad has always prided himself on his memory for telephone numbers, but now he has no need of it. Another thing to relinquish. He puts on a couple of kilos and is euphoric. He makes a trip to his unit with Justin to get a few items of clothing and water his roses. He doesn't mention returning permanently, but later Amanda says he did suggest to her that perhaps, just perhaps, he might be able to go back for Christmas. Hope wheedles in, but then we're told his extra kilos are all fluid, and he must go to hospital to have his lungs drained.

'These things happen,' he says, but he sounds small and distant, and it isn't the new phone.

I rejoin the falcons. If Dad can keep calm and carry on, so can I. The three large teenagers, all prance and pomp in their near-adult bodies, glare into my teary eyes with disdain. *Get a grip*, they seem to be saying. *We sleep on top of each other in the place where we shit and kill. You're weak. Pathetic.*

Runty hangs back, devoid of judgement. In fact, Runty seems absent, even though he's visible. He retreats, as though fearful he might be next, while the others hold down a wattlebird, squabbling for their share. Their killing frenzy is matched by the flap-flap of their wings, and Runty huddles against the wall, as though he could be blown away by their gusts.

I search for information to explain his frailty and learn there are other watchers around the world, knowledgeable people who don't endow birds with human emotions. Runty has become something of a star, but for the wrong reason. Then I find these words on a public Facebook page:

> As people will have noticed the remaining nestling (a male) is struggling . . . From my experience it is most likely a heavy *Trichomoniasis* infection. This is not uncommon in urban and industrial settings where introduced prey species make up a higher proportion of the diet. It is now too late to intervene and approach the ledge as this is guaranteed to lead to this nestling jumping off . . .
>
> As it becomes increasingly obvious that the disease is progressing, I will be recommending to switch off the live feed. Little will be gained by watching its last hours or days.

So Runty will die in privacy. Will he be alone, or will his family gather around him for his final breaths? Will it be fast or slow, in pain or fading into sleep. I won't know if he chooses to make that terrible plunge. Perhaps it's best, but I sob when the feed is turned off, hearing Hamlet's words again: *a special providence in the fall of a sparrow . . .*

Runty was not a sparrow, but he was unique, and the great winged thing got him, despite our vigilance. Inconsolable, I walk in circles around my home, weeping for a little bird that never flew, checking and rechecking websites for some miraculous reprieve.

Peter's death was posted on Facebook before I had even landed in Melbourne that first chilly morning. I was outraged to learn it was in the digital ether, being made more and more real with every 'share'. It was an affront each time someone said they 'had seen', as though his death were a meme.

I check the falcons' website, but there's only a notice suggesting I come back next year. I return nonetheless, just as I went back repeatedly to Peter's dictionary and coffee mug.

We continue to wait for a 'vacancy' for Dad. I send emails to jog bureaucratic memories; their seahorses are overworked, stressed and grossly underpaid. I search for words that will form themselves into something, but ability flew with Runty. I impose new delivery dates on myself, and re-number drafts.

deadline
. . . a line beyond which a prisoner dared not go, for fear of being shot

I set up my computer at the dining table, because Runty died in my office, just as Peter died in Amanda's bedroom, and am about to make tea when an almighty thump shakes the windows.

I look up, but there's nothing to see. Then I hear it. A lorikeet. Their high-pitched chatter is part of the everyday soundscape, but this is different. It's a single forlorn note, wailed over and over, silencing even the magpie chicks.

It's on the balcony railing, leaning forward, craning its brilliant blue head, before retracting it to make that eerie cry. It leans forward, pulls back; leans forward again, almost toppling, then back. It tilts its head, the bright red beak opening and closing.

I step towards the window. Too late to unsee, I understand. Lying motionless on the tiles is another lorikeet, its orange, yellow and green feathers unmoving, and a trickle of murky liquid under its neck. The living bird—its mate?—continues, back and forward, but now I'm doing it, too.

'No,' I say as tears come. 'No. No.'

The survivor's bright eye looks into mine. *I didn't do it*, I want to say. *This was not my fault.* I have no idea whether to intervene or to allow space. Should I pick up the body? What? What?

The kettle. Quick. Flick it on, grab the pot, find the leaves. Breathe. The squawks follow me. Do something. Do something.

'I'm making tea,' I say, as I open the cupboard.

The milk jug is cinched at the middle, as though corseted. 'Hips' and 'waist' are decorated with yellow roses, symbolising friendship, and blue forget-me-nots, that signify true love or remembrance after death. It's a sentimental utensil that belonged to my grandmother, then my mother. When she died, it came to me. Very little else did. There was a dress ring (now remade, combined with my wedding and engagement rings), a favourite horseriding shirt and her weighty photo album. She knew time was running down, so she sorted in advance. By the time of her death, her possessions fitted into two suitcases, as though she were going on a cruise.

Mysteriously, the milk jug survived. I kept it but never used it. When, years ago, I dropped it onto the tiled floor of our shack, I cried.

'I don't even like it,' I said, tears plopping onto the shattered fragments.

'Go for a walk,' Peter said. 'Go on.'

I stormed into the hot morning, berating myself for my stupidity in not realising the jug carried history, regardless of its aesthetics. I wept and walked, remembering Ning and Mum in kitchens where they'd made tea and drop scones.

Mum and my stepfather bought a farm when I was about six. It was the first home they'd made together, and Alanna was born there. They worked hard and long, but money was elusive, and eventually they had to sell. A potential buyer came to inspect the place, and as he sat in the kitchen waiting for the kettle to boil, he quizzed Mum.

'Do you have any problems with snakes?' he asked.

'No, none at all,' she replied, opening the crockery cupboard.

There, on the shelf below the cups and saucers and Ning's milk jug, lay a coiled Stimson's python. Quick as a flash, Mum grabbed her rifle and shot it. No problem. She selected a teapot, closed the cupboard and went back to the conversation. Incredibly, the man bought the farm and the jug survived.

When I returned to our shack, I was red of cheeks, eyes and nose but prepared to scrape the jug's remnants into the bin.

'An object doesn't contain a person's story,' I announced to Peter.

He thought otherwise.

'There you are,' he said. 'Good as new.'

The jug stood on the kitchen bench, flawless, as though time had reversed to the moment before the drop. I went to pick it up, but—

'Let it set,' he said. 'It will be fine.'

Of course he had superglue. He was a fixer, like Dad, with extra light globes and spare fuse wire at the ready. I never had bandaids or string; I resisted the idea that things break or fall apart. But now I keep masking tape and sewing kits, blu-tack and sealant, and the jug is a treasure. It doesn't come out of the cupboard, but when I see its hairline cracks, I remember the tenderness that bound it back together. That jug was an unloved thing, then a broken thing, but it became a thing of beauty when Peter repaired it.

The kettle boils. I fill the pot and locate an old red handtowel while tea steeps. (I know, Pete—steep like a hill?—weird word.)

I slide open the glass door. The living lorikeet flaps and squawks as I enfold the inert bird in the towel and pick it up. Its turquoise head lolls, the yellow-tipped beak contrasting with the towel. The bird on the railing shrieks and bobs, its calls frantic, so I wrap the towel tighter and stand, feeling the weight of death. Other birds have flown away or fallen silent, but the survivor's keening fills the sky. Don't tell me creatures don't mourn. This one is agonised.

Carrying the towel-shroud, I go inside, and I walk downstairs, and I consider bin or burial, and I remember Peter digging that enormous hole for our darling dog, and how we ran out of tea that day, and how he sobbed and I couldn't offer comfort; and I remember his ashes blowing onto my bare legs, and how there was a conversation with the funeral director about it being lucky (lucky?) he wanted to be cremated because some burials had not been possible through the heavy rains of that Melbourne winter because the ground was too wet and people were waiting in queues to be dug into the earth and graves were subsiding, and I had forgotten all that until now, as I hold the heavy-but-nothing body of the bird that has woken up my internal seahorses.

Over the road is a patch of bush. I creep off the track, wattles and spiky shrubs scratching my bare arms and legs, and set down the bundle. I scrape the sandy soil and bawl as my hands dig and dig, and I should have brought a shovel, but of course I don't have one, and my fingers hurt but I keep on digging until I have made a place for the body, and I lay it in the ground and cover it over and pat the earth and wipe my eyes and I know I've smeared my face but I don't care as I sit back on my haunches, straining for breath. Which fool said a bird in the hand is worth two in the bush?

There is a lorikeet to my left, a metre away. It steps forward, bobs its head, steps back, bobs, then steps forward again, and I don't know if it is grieving or grateful, or if it even knows what I've done, because I don't know whether it's the same one, but somewhere in me I know, and I don't care what scientists say, I know this bird has been felled by grief, and that days will never be the same. Not ever . . .

Is this what it was like for Runty's parents?

Months later, I will learn that his mother picked him up after he died and took him away from the nest. Perhaps it was an instinct to keep the space clean of disease. Maybe it didn't want the remaining siblings to see—or, worse, to eat—the corpse. Or was it just a wish to mourn, alone, the death of a child?

The lorikeet keeps up its two-step. I want to shoo it away, to tell it to get on with life, but it hops forward, back, forward, back. Right foot in and right foot out, but no rightness anywhere.

I cross the road, bin the red towel, mount the stairs and scrub my hands until they throb. I carry my mug of tea onto the balcony. To my right, on the tiles, is a dark stripe of liquid. I sip tea, waiting for the panic to subside. I'm not ready to deal with red stains.

Days pass. There is voice work. Income. Dad says he's feeling better, despite still being in that ward. There are rumours of his border opening for Christmas. We dare to hope.

A friend dies in Melbourne, but I don't hear until after the funeral. I last saw her when she and her partner came to visit, not long after I moved here. They'd been together for forty years, Bea told me, and Jay nodded when her eyes flitted to his for confirmation. She had the beginnings of dementia but still remembered important things like poetry and the botanical names of plants.

'How lovely are these?' she said, clapping her hands at the enormous bunch of flowers they'd given me. 'Aren't you decadent to have so many?'

Jay laughed and agreed. His patience was tender and protective, but also studded with gentle humour, so Bea was never reduced. I boiled the kettle while she wandered the room, touching leaves and saying names.

Acacia pycnantha.

Antirrhinum majus.

Agave amica.

She stroked the new tips, instructing me on which ones might need fertiliser. 'Pete will have some, of course, darling. Where is he? There won't be any cake left if he doesn't come soon.'

I looked to Jay, lost for a reply.

He took Bea's hands. 'Pete's dead, darling. I'm sorry. I should have reminded you. It's alright. Really, now, it's alright. Don't worry.'

She was ashamed, desperate to apologise—and she was grief-stricken. I watched her face crumple at the news, her body deflating and tears welling. It was as though Peter had died right then. I saw in her face what it was like for me that first night: all life, all air, gushing from the body. Life, exiting stage left.

When she calmed, we spoke of Peter. She recited some Yeats. '*I shall have some peace there, for peace comes dropping slow . . .*'

I'd always believed those words were inscribed on me like markings in stone after Peter recited them to me at places we visited in Ireland, yet as I listened, I couldn't recall more than a phrase or two. But here was Bea, losing her life's history yet remembering every word. The hippocampus is wayward.

After they left, I cleared plates and tipped out tea-leaves, wiped surfaces and washed dishes, all traces of them gone. I wondered if that was how Bea's memory worked—or whether she was only losing sad stuff.

I've wondered that about myself. My memories tend to accentuate the positive of the good people I've known and to sharpen the hard lines of those I've found to be cruel. I don't sanctify anyone—I can see that Mum was wilful, and that Peter's anxiety was a wall that sometimes neither of us could see over or through—but I think my memories enlarge the essential qualities of those I've lost. Now, when I think of Bea, I recall her faith—in God and humans—and the gentleness that belied her deep, booming voice.

In late November, a new coordinator joins the staff of the little place we've selected for Dad. She suggests they give him a single room at their sister site—a place he'd considered too posh— while we wait for a permanent vacancy. After seven weeks of 'boarding school', he will be able to sleep through. He can spread out a few belongings and have a private bathroom. I'm ecstatic at this kindness, particularly because the border opening is looking less and less imminent.

A date is set for the move. It's next week. Brett buys new clothes for Dad and they're tagged with his name.

It's the day after tomorrow. He's excited. He's ready. He's grateful.

And he gets shingles.

He has given up his car, his home, his ability to shop and cook and buy a lottery ticket with his paper, his daily wine, his personal agency—even his fags, mostly. And now, itching and burning, after all that loss, he must be isolated in the world's most isolated city. I don't have Bea's faith, and I could murder the gods for doing this to him.

The coordinator could not be more compassionate. Yes, they will hold his place. Everyone is gentle and reasonable, but Dad has shingles and must be locked up all alone. I still can't get across that bloody border, and nothing seems just. Where, oh where, is the god for me to slay?

Clocks tick. Days stretch and minutes slow. I don't go out or see people, except those at the beach or on my walking paths. It's as though I've locked down again in solidarity with Dad. I ride a ferry to the city and back one day, telling myself it's research, but it only accentuates the sense that I'm moving but going nowhere.

I rearrange still lifes in my home, placing a dark sea urchin inside a nest I found over a year ago, during our first lockdown. The fallen home seemed like a manifestation of all my fears for those I loved. Now, I snuggle it against my grandfather's pocket watch with its stilled hands.

In Marina's pictures, time is frozen. Dahlias stay sculptural and cherry blossoms never lose petals. Lucien Henry's waratah picture has a bet each way—the petals and crown of the bloom are all crimson youth , but leaves have fallen. The end approaches, they suggest.

In a genre known as vanitas, artists caution us about our transience. Hourglasses, wilted flowers and guttering flames warn that time is fleeting; that we are dying even as we admire the beauty inside the frame. Grasp life, they urge. Wriggle for it.

The Latin word *vanitas* means futility or worthlessness. Those paintings warn of impermanence, insisting against attachment to things of this world—even to milk jugs and dictionaries and those we love. The word comes from the Book of Ecclesiastes: *vanity of vanities; all is vanity . . . One generation passeth away, and another generation cometh; but the earth abideth forever.*

Peter wasn't convinced the earth would abide. There were too many signs—*eustasy*, perhaps—that it was changing irreversibly. I didn't know it on that first morning, but at his funeral, his sister would read from Ecclesiastes.

To everything there is a season . . .

I LOCATE THE word on page 375.

deicide

1. *the killer of a god*
2. *the killing of a god*

On that page, Peter marked the word *deforestation.* No surprise in that. But he also marked parts of the entry for Daniel Defoe, and I can't be sure what appealed to him most about it . . . *secret service work . . . Robinson Crusoe . . .*

At the end of the entry, I find the title of another book: *A Journal of the Plague Year.*

It has already been more than a year, Pete. Almost two plague years, now. What if it never ends? What if they never let me see Dad again?

It's impossible to get information. It's hard to know who to trust. The virus is killing off the gods of science, along with our elders. We can't tell what is real and what is false. You haven't heard about fake news, Pete. I'm glad you've missed that.

Glad?

No.

I feel no gladness. Just the weight of waiting.

DAD IS FREED from solitary.

He moves to his third temporary nest, in the posh place. It's like a hotel, he says, but peopled with high-care patients who have little or no conversation. Still, he has his own room at last and, with the help of his wheelie-walker, can take the lift down to chat to the reception staff. They unlock the glass doors so he can smoke on the footpath.

He's near Justin, even if he is on the corner of two six-lane roads. Not to worry; it's silent inside, he reassures me. He makes the best of everything, describing the variety of passing cars— once you were either a Ford or Holden person, he says—and speculating on the future of electric vehicles. He still yearns to get back behind the wheel of his Falcon—most reliable engine ever made, that one. When I was a tot, he raced cars for a few seasons, and the annual 'best' edition of *Wheels* magazine is his marker of changing times and technology.

Perth's summer is flexing its muscles. Dad has aircon but insists on going into the blazing sun for his 'smoko'. He is not a child. I will not worry. Instead, I book a flight to see Alanna and Amanda. The border between our states has opened and we've decided that, since it's unlikely we'll get to Perth, I will come south for a pre-Christmas visit.

On 11 December, as the plane circles Melbourne, I peer at city buildings, trying to locate the peregrines' home. It's almost a month since the live stream was switched off. Runty would now be nothing but feathers and bones. His siblings will be wide-winged regents of the skies.

I hug my sisters and raise glasses with Peter's clan. I walk with friends around the Botanic Gardens, relaxing into shaded glades and shared history. The serene order of the city's green spaces is balm. The gallery's water wall welcomes me with misty rainbows, and when I stop outside our old home, I am grateful to see that it has had a lick of paint. Once, I might have resented any change to it, but now, as the car idles and I scan the facade, I am grateful it is loved.

Our little dog will be pushing up flowers in the back garden and, not for the first time, I think how it would be good to be laid into the earth naked, like him and the lorikeet, rather than being burned or going into the ground clothed and inside a box. I think about becoming food for worms, then magpies and crows, becoming blood and bone for an angophora or a birch to thrive and grow, and I almost envy that little dog.

Almost. Only almost. I actually feel no envy or pain as I roam the streets and the bay, alone or in company, remembering, in the warm of early summer. Small tender details of our life rise like the persistent daisies that push through cracks in pavements. Memory is no longer a drama queen, attached to the big tragic moments. Instead, she is humble, offering up snapshots on every corner, and they are kind, nourishing and reassuring.

Alanna's home, where she has spent so much time locked down alone, is no longer a sanctuary. Not a prison, she insists, but maybe a cage. We see a place online—it's high up and looks out to the city and bay and, amazingly, it's affordable, so we inspect it together. She is uncertain, because it's in the same building as Amanda and her partner and his daughter, just two floors up, and she will be too close for all of their comfort, and will feel she is stalking them, and—

They allay her fears. I push her, because I remember how I felt when the home I'd loved was no longer my refuge. She stays a night in my high-rise serviced apartment, and on waking we watch hot-air balloons drifting across the skyline. I can't see any falcons, but she can see a way forward. She decides she wants a nest instead of her cave, so she applies, and on my last morning she's told she has it. My sisters will be under the same roof, able to visit each other in pyjamas and stockinged feet, to be there as backstop if a curveball is thrown.

I fly out on 17 December. I'm once again looking down, but now things are looking up. For the first time since Peter died, our shared city has been all joy. I'm grateful. Melbourne is still a home.

I'm welcomed to my other home by a persistent cockatoo. He perches on my kitchen windowsill banging his metallic beak against the window. When I tell him to go away, he squawks, almost tipping himself off the ledge, but then rights himself and begins his rat-a-tat-tat again. It's only when I laugh at him that he leaves, tipping and dipping, an indignant drunken roisterer.

I wander to the water and plunge, floating over seahorses and urchins. As I hang out my towel, two kookaburras chorus from the eucalypt. The sun dips, and I call Dad, who is delighted to hear about the Melbourne trip. He's tending the indoor plant I sent him for Father's Day and is chuffed that he can still get things to grow, even in a 'facility'.

He tells me Santa came to visit the residents, and although it was a bit silly—*He must have been forty years younger than me, honey, and I think he felt a bit embarrassed when he asked me what I'd like for Christmas*—he had a good chat with him because, after all, everybody needs to earn a living. Afterwards, Dad says, he realised he should have admitted that he did have a wish: for his daughters to be able to cross the border soon.

We're getting closer, I tell him. So is Christmas.

EVERYTHING IS WHITE, but it can't be snow. Not at Christmas.

Drifting. It's mid-afternoon by now, surely.

Pain. There was pain, and codeine. I tried to read. More codeine. More codeine. Cold then hot, shivering. My head exploding.

Was this what it was like, Peter? With no warning?

I had warning. I had a week of pain, after Melbourne, in my brain and down my right side. Tectonic plates shifting. Head erupting down the right side. No, wrong. All down the wrong side, which is the right side and is still the wrong side. Pain and a kind of animal moaning, and birds on the balcony, feathered things squawking, coming for me, that feathered thing, yours, black and glossy with extended claws, and codeine and more codeine and more pain.

Is this it, Pete? Is it my turn now?

I called triple zero. A seahorse must have woken up and given me the number. So they were not damaged. I hope.

You took how many tablets? Since when? How many? Get the packet and tell me again.

Ambulance. Coming. They will come. Turn things off. Electricity. Can you do that?

Yes.

Kind, they are kind as I sob and shake.

Pain.

Now, now, the voice says, everything is under control. Now, now . . .

They do come. In uniforms. A uniform makes everything better. They have uniforms and a thing to wrap tight around my arm. Put a needle in. And another. Ask me whatever you want and I will tell. Anything to stop the pain.

They note what drugs I've taken and they walk me down the stairs and put a paper bracelet on my arm—there, there—not a paper hat for Christmas, and my neighbour of the magpies puts her head into the ambulance and her mouth makes a perfect O—it's a word, I want to tell the paramedics—and we leave, and I am wishing them Merry Christmas and apologising for taking away their turkey and they are kind and it seems I will not be like you, Pete, and I don't know if that is good or bad.

Now, now, they say as I try to tell them about you. They said it was like a hammer to the head, I tell them. Now, now, they say. Now, now, now . . .

Casualty. Emergency. Fast-track. Morphine.

What? No, no, I don't need—

Oh, it creeps and, oh, it crawls under my skin, I tell the nurse, and she smiles and says now, now, surely not, but I can, I can, I can feel a slow train coming down my veins. It is cool and for a moment I think we might leave the station but no . . .

No. The pain. The right side. It stops at the centre of my jaw, at my front teeth, the left side is free. I don't understand. What? What?

Now, now, now . . .

Lyrica.

Mobic.

Carbamazepine.

They try all of these. Paracetamol, too.

Endone. End. One. I don't want to end . . . Sometimes I thought I did but now I know I don't.

There are feathers, angels, featherfoots, falcons, wings, flying, ravens, diving, soaring, feathers, beaks, eyes, pipping, pip-pip-pipping . . .

My head hurts but not like before. The cannula in my arm twinges. On a scale of one to ten, how is the pain? What is one? Kicking my toe? What is ten?

It was eleven.

Now maybe eight. Relief like rain.

The arm hurts. The cannula can't feel. It doesn't feel anything, the cannula.

No. No real pain. There is shadow pain, a thing that might sink its talons into my ear and jaw and temples, and squeeze like it could rip inside. A glossy night-dark feather-memory . . .

I don't think it's hurting. I can't tell. Everything is screaming and noise, but maybe that's outside me, here in emergency. It's no longer in my head or my brain or my mind or whatever it is we are going to call it. We never did work that out, Pete, did we?

I'm scared. Pump the drugs in. Keep them coming. Don't leave me with it again. I speak to Alanna and she tells me I am going to be alright . . .

I don't know how that happened. How did she find me?

In the next cubicle a doctor is examining a young woman. I saw her roll past on another gurney. Is that what they're called, Pete, or is that only in movies?

Gurney. Journey. Attorney. Herni-a. What else?

The girl laughs and the doctor tries again. I strain to hear. I want to understand. Something. Anything. Merry Christmas.

'You were on a boat. Your friends brought you here. You blacked out.'

'Good friends,' she says.

'Please lie still,' the doctor says. 'I need you to answer some questions.'

'Sure. Make them easy though'—she laughs—'I hate quizzes.'

Puggles, I want to call to her. They won't get that.

'Can you tell me if you were drinking?'

'When?'

'On the boat.'

'Oh. Then. Well . . . yeah,' she answers. 'Yeah, of course.'

'How many drinks might you have had?'

'I dunno. A few . . . Maybe six or seven cocktails.'

'Excellent,' the doctor says. She has won the quiz. 'Any drugs?'

'Just a few lines . . .'

I want to close my eyes, but if I do the pain might find me.

A hammer to the back of the head . . . bang bang, smash smash, down he went . . .

I don't want to go with you, Pete. I'm sorry. I want to be here, on the solid side of the fence. I want to be on the balcony reading my Christmas book, which is about dragons and skin and Weet-Bix. I don't want to be remembering. Red stains on pillowcases. Yuletide red and white. Crumpled sheets. I don't want to be with you there. I don't.

Traitor.

I sleep. I wake. It's dark. Am I dead? Is this it, Pete?

Maybe this is the morgue . . . maybe I'm a body on a tray in the fridge.

That isn't funny. It's not. So stop smirking.

Dad isn't going out because it's over forty degrees. They told me that yesterday. I didn't get to say Merry Christmas, because it was too early over there when my ambulance came. And there was pain. And codeine. I wanted to vomit for pain.

But Dad will be alone. He went in an ambulance, too, but that was two months ago. No. Two months and two weeks. I can still do sums.

I made my bed while I was waiting for the people in uniforms. Just in case. So my sisters would not find disarray if they came. No rumpled sheets. No vomit stains. My will on the left-hand corner of my desk. Pyjamas folded behind the pillows. I sleep in pyjamas now. I don't want anyone to walk in on my naked sprawl; to see my body, limbs skewed like a discarded doll's.

No. Not that.

Is that how he was?

Open your eyes. Open your eyes.

For the first time in days the pain is not married to aloneness. When the morphine went into my arm, I was a pipe and I could feel the gushing to the tap and I was not married to aloneness anymore. I was not alone. I am not alone. I don't give a shit about cranberries or mistletoe, because my head is not going to burst while these nurses are here. Close by. Keeping watch. I am not alone. The nurses at the station smile when I catch their eye. They are close. I am not alone.

Not like he was.

Not like Dad is.

Forty degrees . . .

———

I sleep.

I wake.

Someone is vomiting.

Nurse Amanda checks my pulse. Another Amanda. I have a sister Amanda, I tell her. And a friend Amanda, who was with me when Peter died. Nurse Amanda does not know who Peter is. Amanda means *worthy of love*, I tell her. She smiles and says she's sorry I must be in emergency for Christmas.

I love her, I tell her. I love her so much. I may be in love with her, I think.

I sleep.

I wake.

Down the corridor, a man keeps retching and laughing, making great engorged vomit sounds. Nurse Amanda takes my temperature and I ask what's wrong.

'He swallowed a piece of steak at Christmas lunch, and it's stuck,' she says. 'Ho ho ho. Heave heave heave.' She winks. 'We nurses always chew our food.'

I love her. I feel safe. Love is feeling safe, I tell her. She says I'm right and pats my arm.

I sleep.

'Any pain?' Nurse Amanda is beside me.

'In the distance. But it feels like it's a long way away now. What time is it?' There are no windows. There is no daylight. No stars. No sky. No birds.

Peter was alone. I am not alone. I have drugs and Nurse Amanda and screaming lunatics and a coked-up kid who doesn't know she has fallen on her head. These are my people. I am not alone.

I sleep.

I wake.

I don't know if my mind is to be trusted. My brain. My head. My . . . what is it, Peter?

A doctor—or a nurse?—tells me the brain is just meat, but the mind is magic.

I want to stay here forever. I don't want to go home.

Where is home? Where is Peter?

I haven't told him. I haven't told my sisters. Or have I? I talked to Alanna. She is my next of kin. Or is it kith? Or both? Is she my home?

Peter is gone. Alanna is in Melbourne with our other sister Amanda. Did I tell her I am here? I ask Nurse Amanda. So many Amandas. So much love.

I had a book. There was a book. The ambulance people should have told me to bring the book. Bring a toothbrush, they said. And your phone charger. All I need for the end of the world. Clean teeth. A charged telephone.

But the book is Christmas.

My seahorses dance, and I remember . . .

I went yesterday to the bookshop. I picked up a parcel. I have a book about a dragon. It's at home, on the table. I am here, on a trolley, a Christmas turkey, on a gurney. On a wheelie thing, like Dad has a wheelie-walky thing . . .

'Well,' the doctor says, whisking back the curtains, 'Merry Christmas. You're in strife, aren't you?'

She is lean, like an athlete, and her eyes are bright and sharp, like a falcon. She has none of the weary staleness of the others. She is new-minted, born on Christmas Day, like Jesus the Saviour, following my star. She asks me to repeat my litany, and when I tell her I had been near fainting, near vomiting, and when I tell her how many painkillers I have taken, she whistles.

'Alright then, Jingle Bells, let's see if we can figure this out for you.' She turns to go but then looks back.

'Do you live alone?'

I nod. 'But I have sisters in Melbourne,' I say. 'And brothers in Perth. And a father.'

She is gone, like a mother peregrine, gone to get food for chicks. I hear her in the next cubicle. 'Wait there,' she says. 'I'll be back.' She flits in and out, her voice a chirrup. I want to squawk after her. *Bring drugs! Bring drugs!*

I roll over, mouth dry, pain down my right side, but no stab, no fear, only dullness and barf, barf, retch, retch from the vomiter down the corridor. Steak still stuck. Still-stuck-steak. I say it three times. A twister for my thick, drugged tongue.

He is trying, like a parent bird, to cough up meat, but he's not made for it.

I am watched. There is no webcam, but they come and go, and it's night and then day, somewhere in the world, but here it is only night-day or day-night, and I think I am showered, but I am still in emergency and I cry on the phone to Alanna that it's crazy here, and she says now, now, they will find me a bed in a ward, and Nurse Amanda comes. She has done two full day shifts, into the night, and still she is on duty because Covid is slaying all of her team, and she brings me a chicken sandwich, which she has had to hunt down elsewhere in the hospital, because they don't normally keep people in emergency this long and don't have food options for patients, so please eat it, and I want to vomit in symphony with Steak Man but she says I have to eat it, with all the drugs rampaging, and so I bite into bird flesh.

I tell Amanda that a group of feeding vultures is called a wake, but she just says to eat up. I want to tell her how, at first, the hatchlings were like furry pancakes. When they were hungry, a head would pop up, breaking the soft surface, then collapse again into its siblings. I tell her I watched them on a screen and later she brings me a computer on a trolley. She places it beside my bed and says to look, and she clicks play.

'Now,' Amanda says, 'look at this.'

It's the Queen of England and she is talking.

'There you go,' Amanda says. 'It's her Christmas message. You didn't get turkey or crackers, but at least I can give you that. Happy Boxing Day.' And she is gone again.

I love her more.

I sleep.

I wake.

Have I slept?

I spoke to Alanna. I did. She is telling people. She is the point of contact and the next of kin. She is mine. I put a picture of the corridor in front of my gurney on Instagram. Sunset hour, but there's only neon and white and mess. I turn off comments.

I sleep.

I wake.

Like the chicks. They slept and woke and grew fat and their cries grew more insistent. *Bring me! Bring me!* And the parents killed and killed for them.

And Runty died. Runty fell. Or did he? No. I fell. I should have told them. I fell. But that was two years ago. Do they need to know? Amanda. Amanda . . .

They try me on other drugs. Amanda, apologetic, says I must stay here in emergency, because there are no beds in neurology.

Neurology?

What's happening?

Haemorrhage?

No, that was Peter. They never said that word to me. They never said eustasy either. Or lenticular. I could murder some lentils.

The pain breaks through but when I press a button someone comes. 'Maybe we'll try some Lyrica again.'

I don't care. They are there, these adult peregrines, fussing about me and filling me full of the good stuff.

My third chicken sandwich sticks in my throat.

I sleep.

I wait.

I will be two nights and three days in emergency, in vomiting cursing craziness, as nurses tend and doctors flit, coats swishing behind them, and the lights stay on and the observations continue and I am the chick in the nest and Amanda, Nurse Amanda, comes and goes, comes and goes, bringing and checking, a mother bird under fluorescent lights.

I am not alone. I am mad, but I am not alone. I am in a bed, but it is not a deathbed. I weep, but I'm not alone. I don't know what day it is, or what these drugs are, but I'm not alone . . .

They move me to a ward. There are four of us, just like Dad for all that time. I'm beside a window, and I can see down six or seven storeys from my new nest. A dropping of pigeons flies past at eye level; they even perch from time to time. It's quiet. I text my sister coherent messages—or more coherent, at least. In the grey of dawn, a friend walks past on the street with his new baby girl in a pouch on his back, and they wave up to me.

I shower. I am drugged but stable. I take slow walks up and down corridors. I speak to Connaught, in the bed beside me.

Soon, she says, they will move her to palliative care. She has been here for weeks, not allowed a visitor because of Covid. She has not told her children she's dying, because she didn't want to ruin Christmas. I listen when she finally calls them, one at a resort and the other interstate and unable to fly into Sydney. She is calm and firm, and when they ask her why she didn't tell them, she says this is how she has always managed things. Her way.

'If they do let you come across the border, you can stay in my place,' she tells the younger one. 'It's your inheritance, after all. But the sheets will need changing.'

Afterwards, she lies looking at the ceiling. I perch on her bed and we hold hands. She is all bones and crepe-thin skin, but her dark eyes look right into me.

'That must have been hard,' I say.

'It's done,' she says. 'Now they can move me. I didn't want to go until I'd told them.' She will be taken over the road, to the hospice. They will have to get permission for her to have a visitor.

'Will you be okay, not having family around?'

'Just fine,' she says. 'I want to be on my own for this.'

'You're not scared?'

'No. No, I've had time to get used to it. And I don't like pain.'

She grips my hand; squeezes it. She manages a small smile. 'The thing they don't tell you is that it's interesting, Ailsa. You, of that strong Scottish name, called after that big dark rock in the middle of the sea . . . you might understand that. It's interesting, this dying.'

I sit for a few more moments, then she drifts back to sleep. I wait until her hand lets go of mine, and then totter out to the corridor so she can't see my tears. She has reminded me that I am named for Ailsa Craig, a formidable black island of rock, shaped a little like Uluru. It's in the channel between Ireland and Scotland and is a bird sanctuary, home to massive numbers of gannets and, more recently, puffins. Birds and angels . . . and are there serpents, I wonder?

Like Peter, my name is rocky.

Like Peter, Connaught will die alone.

Is it possible Peter could have found death interesting?

They are packing her belongings. It takes only minutes. Nurses come to wish her well—she has been with them longer than most. I have known her only a day but will never forget her.

The doctors speak to me the next morning. They tell me they still don't really know what's causing the pain—not for sure—but the drugs that are working suggest it's a condition called trigeminal neuralgia. I don't much care so long as the pain is not breaking through, but I sit up and take notice when they tell me my MRI result showed an aneurysm on my left carotid artery. It's just a chance finding, they say, because the neuralgia is on the right, but they have found it and now they will need to watch it. I will need to watch it.

Aneurysm.

A word I won't look up. My brother's wife died from one. My stepmother died from one. Peter had a brain haemor-rhage, his blood pushing through one fragile membrane. A bloodburst.

This is not good, but the drugs kick in and I roll over and sleep.

Rolling over and sleeping will become my new normal. This is the gift of the drugs. I will also grow skilled at sitting and staring at the horizon. I learn to totter, because I'm told, when they discharge me, that I will be a fall risk for a while, due to the medication I must continue to take.

I get home in time for New Year, but I'm asleep as the clock ticks over, and I don't notice any change on rising. 'Now' is now 2022. Another new normal.

For an elongated blurry month, everything is slow motion or no motion. I observe the tree canopy for hours. I look up, never down, after the first time I lean over and feel a powerful tug to fall. I wonder whether Runty was ever drawn to the edge. I make sure my chair is pushed back, far from that seductive drop.

The eucalypt blossoms smell like honey, and the drone of fat sassy bees is loud and continuous. Lorikeets feast and feud, their greedy shrieking penetrating the bee buzz. I speak to Dad every day in the sweet silence of the afternoon. It is hot on both sides of the continent, but he has more energy than I do.

A neighbour takes me to the beach each morning, so I don't trip. We meander, slowly, slowly through the steamy streets, remarking on the variety of weatherboard cottages and paint colours. We swim slowly, slowly at the cove, because it's too far to the seahorses. I see silvery slivers of life and, one memorable morning, horseshoe-shaped jellyfish on the sand. I tell my neighbour they are the egg sacs of moon snails and, very gently, I lift one of them back into the water and watch it float away. Zoologist Liz writes that there are rose-petal bubble snails down on the rocks, and I look for them but can't find their wing-like flaps. I tell Dad about them and he laughs. If a rose-petal snail got into his garden it wouldn't last long, he says.

Each afternoon, in the distance I hear an ice-cream van.

Greensleeves was all my joy . . .

I think it's memory playing tricks, but then I learn it's real.

Trying to fathom reality is an ongoing game, along with trying to stay awake. The drugs stupefy my hippocampi. Past and present blur.

The van comes most days, and I sing that line, then mean to seek out other lyrics, but I forget what I was searching for by the time I get to the computer. One day Dad hears it in the background and says when I was little I would never let an ice-cream van pass by.

Each morning I play Wordle, a new online anagram game, exchanging results with five sets of friends. Dad isn't interested in it, insisting he's a pen and paper guy, but I'm sure Peter would have succumbed.

Sure? Let's not go overboard.

Chums visit, bringing food and stories of their days and the books they're reading, and we sit and toddle and swim slowly . . . the days slow . . . my reading slows . . . my speech slows. I am a snail, waiting on my rock. A weak peregrine on a concrete ledge, with the buzz of bee life as a soundtrack.

Dad waits, too. In his temporary posh air-conditioned digs, he sits out a scorching western summer, going downstairs for a cigarette then coming in from the heat, panting. Our days move at the same pace. I'm still an outlaw, unable to get permission to cross that border, but I would be unable to do anything other than wait anyway, while the drugs do their work.

My birthday comes, and my friend who wrote the cloud-covered book feeds me a home-cooked dinner. The Elegant Backstroker gives me a bracelet with the word *HOPE* inscribed on it. Maybe this really is home. Maybe these people are my anchors.

anchor
a thing affording stability

You didn't mark that word, Pete. You marked another on the same page. I can't imagine why it appealed to you.

anchorite

a hermit; a religious recluse; a person of secluded habits

That's me, waiting in white-out that is blinding sun but could be snow. Waiting in my nest but not incubating anything, not pipping, just sitting . . .

Then, on 4 February, Dad moves into his permanent placement.

home

There are so many definitions, Pete—dozens of entries—and you haven't marked one of them. It's my favourite word in the English language, with that soft 'oh' sound at its heart, even though I am never sure where my home is located. Will I ever have a forever home? Is this it? It was Peter once, but now?

Oh, I say. Oh, oh, Dad is home. I could weep for relief, but also for dread. Now reality must set in.

He has a small room looking into an internal courtyard, and he says it's just fine, darling, don't you worry now, you just get well. They will open the border eventually. You will see it soon. There are birds for me to watch, he says, and there are roses. It's just fine.

I long to make beauty and comfort for him, but I remain locked out. My brothers settle him in—some things from his unit, a new recliner chair. The rest, the 'titivating'—marvellous word he uses—can wait until I arrive. It can all wait, he says.

So, I wait, imagining his bones cocooned in velvets and cushions, his body wrapped in plush. The drugs dull my impatience, but I'm relieved when I'm told I can begin to decrease the dosage. It will take weeks, but slowly, slowly my brain (head, mind?) will return to normal functioning.

It will take months, maybe years, to trust that brain again, though, and memories, which were elusive at best, will become objects of suspicion.

I wait for the border to open.

I sleep, like a chick, for hours.

I swim, slow as a seahorse.

I wait for my head to clear.

Now, now, I tell myself when black moods descend.

February crawls on. The hottest month. The slowest month. Now, now.

Just wait.

Eventually, the pipping must come.

Still life with clock
and binoculars

BINOCULARS RECLINED AGAINST the base of a round wooden clock, both backlit by late afternoon sun. The lenses of the binoculars, along with the glass face of the clock, made three mirrors, reflecting the interior of a room and a woman in a grey dress, seated at an unpolished wooden table.

I'd made tea, but the dregs of brew 50,476 were untouched and the day was passing, second by interminable second, on the clock Alanna had given us as a wedding present. It must have ticked more than 920,160,000 times.

Alanna was somewhere in mid-air, hurtling from west to east. My other sister, Amanda, was travelling in China. I had no idea what o'clock it was there. My brothers were two hours behind, in Perth, with Dad. Peter's family were in the here and now but, like me, were lost.

Say what you see. That's how to find your position.

On the table was a vase of irises, the flower he liked best: *Iris latifolia*, which is native to the French Pyrenees, a detail that pleased both of us, because I'd walked across those mountains a couple of times, and he'd waved me off on the French side before collecting me in a warm rental car in Spain.

His laptop—well, my old laptop that he'd inherited—sat like a white tombstone on the pine tabletop, its green light pulsing in time with the clock. Just as the milk jug had outlived Ning and Mum, so the computer had outlived Peter, despite all my warnings that it was dying.

'Just because it's slow doesn't mean it's dead,' he'd replied.

I pushed it away, the gesture snapping me into action. I picked up a business card, left by police, for a cleaning service that specialised in 'situations' like this, and called their office, only to be told that one of their staff members had just learned his son had a brain tumour. There it was again, the winged thing. The woman on the phone sounded wobbly but said she would send someone. It might be late; she couldn't guarantee . . .

Who could?

I picked up his binoculars, fitting them to my eyes. A dove clung to the finial on the roof of his weatherboard studio. I refocused. Birch branches were spindly capillaries against an insipid, bleached sky. A leaf fluttered to the grass. It was just before harvest moon. Fall; time to shed.

———

In the week after Peter's death, I lost five kilos, despite Alanna insisting constantly that I eat. I stopped bleeding, too. Fertility finished.

I worked not to cry, holding myself in, muscles steeled. Sometimes my torso ached so hard I couldn't bend forward. I liked that pain. It felt right. When I did weep, it was in private, and it terrified me. These were like no tears I'd ever shed. They gushed, as though life wanted to flee my body. They were salt but they didn't heal.

It takes roughly twenty-eight days for new skin cells to move through the dermis and epidermis, to become a surface layer called the *stratum corneum*. That's what we let go, every month or so. I've shed over a hundred layers since Peter died.

shed
cause to fall or flow

I tried to imagine him reading the definition to me from page 1333 of his dictionary but couldn't summon his warm tenor. I had recordings of him reading plays and books, documentary narrations and advertising campaigns. I'd listened to him from upstairs and downstairs, across fields and on the next pillow, for nearly three decades. His voice was home, immediately grounding. Why couldn't I remember it?

I called his number.

'*Hi there. You've called Peter. I'm not here right now, but—*'

I hung up.

As darkness arrived, so did a man with a machine like a vacuum cleaner. He was sorry for my loss, he said, as he unloaded pump, hoses and brushes. He suggested I might turn on a heater because the house was freezing. He checked whether someone was coming—*Alanna is coming*—then asked the location of the nearest taps. I showed him the bathroom and scurried away.

Back at the dining table, my gaze turned towards the studio. Its curtains were drawn, as they had been for months. Peter kept that room to and for himself. It was his *shed*; his sanctuary. At some stage I would have to cross its threshold, breaching his privacy. I had not been inside for years. Although we'd been together so long, we kept separate bank accounts and never opened one another's mail. Opening the studio door without his permission would be the first intimation of what was ahead— plundering mobile phone and computer, desk drawers and car pockets, for information. I would be violating his brain (mind, head . . . what?), just as I imagined the coroner was doing at that moment.

The clock ticked on.

I picked up his binoculars, focusing on a painting on the wall opposite, then tilting down to zoom in on the creases in the fabric of the red sofa where he would sit, my first reader, noting typos, repetitions and widow lines, seeking the overlooked thing. Watching Peter read my work was all I needed to know of devotion.

People boast they can read each other like books, but I couldn't predict him. Something was always withheld. Suspense makes you stay the course, with a book or a person, even through the tough stuff. He certainly gave me a surprise ending.

The director of a writers' festival sent me a photograph when she heard he had died. In it, I'm seated, talking to a reader, while Peter stands nearby, watching.

I'm so sad he's gone, she wrote, *when there was so much good living ahead for you both. But what remains is his clear love for you. It's in his tender expression in that chance shot of you signing books.*

Who can say if she was right, but they were kind words. A picture is worth a thousand of them, they say.

I refocused, looking out into the dark. I turned the dials again, but no amount of adjusting allowed me to see a future, so I lay the binoculars back against the clock and watched my own reflection in the window—a motionless fair-haired woman, unaware that for the next six months she would wear nothing but this same grey dress. Mercifully unaware of everything to come.

Through the glass, the teddies seated at the outside table grinned at me.

A few months earlier, Peter had come through the front door with two giant bears, one under each arm. I was appalled— what could he want with these macabre soft toys? He'd rescued them from kerbside rubbish, he said, as he placed them on deckchairs under the bottlebrush tree, declaring they would repel the possums.

For years he'd tried to get rid of those possums. Teddies seemed a ludicrous solution, but he just straightened their velveteen spines, readying them for duty. There they sat, bolt upright, eyes on the paling fence, waiting for night, as I laughed myself to bed. But the flâneur triumphed. The bears terrified the possums. The garden flourished.

The tap man padded down the hall to tell me he was making progress. He worked all the time in such scenes, he said. (Did he call our bedroom a scene?) He had been a forensic detective, but he liked this work better because he was able to feel he had helped—after a loss. He told me that despite my loss, I would be able to sleep there, safe in the knowledge that the room had never been as clean. I wondered whether Mum ever felt she was scouring away sadness or shock, grief or violence.

He went back to work, and I waited while he removed all traces of death. I didn't know, then, how hard it would be to lie in any bed ever again, much less to find sleep in one. All beds would become potential deathbeds.

He reappeared—just checking on me. He said his visit probably had not been necessary, but he understood that I'd been given instructions by the coroner and the police. 'That always happens after a loss at home,' he said, going back to work.

I bristled. Already I resented the suggestion that I'd 'lost' Peter. Say it as it is. He is *dead. No longer alive.*

The man came to say goodbye. He wouldn't charge overtime for working outside office hours, he said. He asked if there was food in the house, and whether I needed anything from the shops. He'd seen them when he turned off the highway, he said, as though I might not know they were there. Perhaps I would like some more tea; he would be happy to make another cup.

'I'm sorry,' I said. 'I didn't get your name.'

'Peter,' he said. 'I'm Peter.'

There were many Peters. As weeks passed, a phalanx of gentle men bearing his name came with spanners and hammers to fix and mend. They were always quiet, solicitous—they were rocks—and I wondered if there was something in the name. I checked, of course.

peter

It meant *to diminish*, the dictionary told me; and *come to an end*, it added for good measure.

After Cleaner Peter left, I stood in the doorway of our bedroom trying to grasp what had occurred. Eventually, I registered something unnerving. There was no smell. Nothing. The scent of our history and our bodies, our clothing and my perfume, was gone. There was no detergent whiff either. Just . . . nothing, no matter how hard I inhaled.

That spooked me. I sprayed eucalyptus and lavender into the air, then made the bed with fresh linen, smoothing its surface as though that gesture could somehow wipe away recent history. I switched on bedside lamps and turned off the overhead. Then I returned to the doorway, at the threshold between normal and crazy.

I scanned the room: a sand-coloured carpet and two matching chests of drawers, each topped by an identical lamp; fireplace to the left, window to the right; the same pictures in the same places. I refocused to close-up—not a speck of dust, not a drop of blood. All was as was, but nothing was as was. I knew right then that I would never sleep on that bed or in that room again.

I whispered, fearful my voice would—what? Wake the dead?

Are you there, Pete?

The clock ticked from the other end of the hall.

I whispered again.

Alanna is coming.

IT'S THE FIRST day of March, and we have permission to cross the border. Any moment I will lift into the sky and wing south to meet my sisters, so we can fly on together to our fathers. I try not to think about my treacherous head or to fret about whether airplane pressure could make the blood vessel pop. My father waits at journey's end. Hurry up. Get this thing airborne before someone tells me I'm an illegal.

It's dawn. Just as it was when I flew to Melbourne after Peter died. We were late then, too, engines thrumming, wings straining. There was a fox on the runway, off to the right. It sniffed the air while planes banked up, unable to take off until the wild thing made its decision. Its red tail bristled; its ears flickered. It was, for those moments, in command of a flock of metal raptors. Then it scarpered out of sight, behind us, and our engines roared, and the great unfeathered bird was untethered, and we rose. As we do now.

Alanna and Amanda meet me at Melbourne airport. We're masked, but our eyes crease into smiles, then tears threaten, so we sit with coffee, sipping furtively, before climbing aboard another metal bird and banking westwards. We are as light as feathers, despite the trepidation. I forget my fears about Covid and aneurysms. I'm safe with my sisters. I will see my father. We are homing.

We're greeted by a phalanx of armed police in full PPE gear. Posing no immediate threat, we are allowed to cab through parched streets to our quarantine rental. We choose rooms and get to work at makeshift desks. In the coming days, we will check our apps and tick every box, joking that the premier is doing drive-bys. We'll obey every rule, obedient starlings, because at the end of this, we will see our fathers. But for now, we will stay in this house, taking our daily rapid antigen test and photographing it on the glass dining table, our bare toes out of focus in the background, before sending it on to anyone who cares.

We rise at 4.30 a.m. to be at work by 5.30 a.m., which is 8.30 a.m. at home. The morning birds here are galahs, like those that fell from the sky in great showers of pink and grey. They skirmish outside our windows, their ungainly feet cracking nuts. They are wild extroverts, celebrating with us and living up to their colloquial name.

Galah: a fool, an idiot.

Justin does a food drop and we talk from behind the door, then play Monopoly Deal and Bananagrams. We tell Dad we're only ten minutes' drive from him now and he sounds chirrupy. We send headshots to the bureaucrats behind the app, to prove we've not left our cage, and then after three days there's a ping on our phones, all of them at once, saying that from tomorrow restrictions will lift, and even we who are quarantining can go free. We toast. We plan. We sleep. Even me, with my fear of bed and bloodburst. I sleep right through the night.

At dawn, I walk to Justin's place, blinking in the unforgiving light, to collect Dad's Falcon. No predator, it's like driving a chugging navy-blue living room on wheels. I return to see Alanna's dad arrive, and photograph them hugging in the driveway, so they can't see I'm crying. There is tea, naturally.

Dad's visiting hours, and numbers, are restricted due to Covid. I've said I will come at 10.30 a.m., after he has breakfasted and showered. Amanda must work, so she will see him in the afternoon. Time creeps. I am restless, tripping over words and forgetting whether I've taken pills. I'm still on medication for the brain. As I wait, my head throbs, then aches, then twitches. There's a buzzing on my left side and floaters in my eyes; a tingle down the right side of my face.

I can't stand it any longer. I start the Falcon and follow directions from my phone, eventually pulling up outside a low-rise cream-brick building, its gardens planted with bottlebrush and grevilleas, where honeyeaters are already at work.

I introduce myself to the staff on the front desk and take a Covid test. While waiting, we chat about weather in Sydney, how long I'm staying—three weeks—and the upcoming football season, but I can't manage small talk. As soon as my timer bleats, I'm off. He's in the Tea-tree section, I'm told: just follow the curving corridor. I have a sense of navigating a maze—will I ever find him?—but finally I locate door thirty-eight. I stop. Inhale. Exhale. And I knock.

His voice is immediately recognisable, so clear and close. 'You're early, sweetheart. Come in.'

And there he is, seated at a high hospital table, the newspaper open to the crossword. Light enters through the glass door behind him, giving him a full-body halo. He rises, smiling. He looks just like himself.

Well, a terribly thin version of himself. He is not masked, but I am. I sanitise, so we can hold hands. We click selfies—a word that amuses him, and which is not in Peter's dictionary—and discuss today's nine-letter word puzzle, an obsession he shared with Pete. We pull apart the news, check the weather and note his urgent need of a haircut. He's in no danger of going bald.

He spots the new bracelet on my right wrist—'Hope springs eternal, darling'—and is chuffed that the silver bangle he gave me for Christmas fifteen months ago is still on my left. He tells a bad Irish joke as I sniff the faintly chemical smell of his room while mentally measuring wall space for furniture. He tells me the food is 'fine' and the staff are 'fine' and the other residents are 'fine'.

The day is also fine, so we take his wheelie chair into the courtyard where crows—'Well, technically, darling, these are ravens, but I still call them crows, too'—magpies and honeyeaters flit from shade sail to roof to garden gnome. Dad tells me the 'ladies' mostly use the courtyard and he is a bit shy about coming outside when they're here, but it's empty now so we take in the cornflower-blue sky, and something unwinds: a click in my head, like a switch.

I'm mesmerised by his hands: the permanent bend of two fingers due to a condition called Dupuytren's contracture; the dry white patches of skin; the blood bruising. They hold a story I've not attended to before—of hard work and embrace, of labour and welcome, and of many a cigarette. No one could call them beautiful, except a daughter who has longed to hold them.

His nails are long, so I trim them. I rub cream into his arms and feet.

'Ahhh,' he sighs, 'aaahh,' closing his eyes and tilting his head to catch more sun.

I note the folds of skin at his neck. He's so very thin. I smooth moisturiser across his forehead and cheeks, and by the time he opens his eyes, mine are free of tears, and I lift the mask so he can see my face properly.

'Your hair's short,' he says.

'It's for swimming.'

He reminds me how he'd walk every morning at Port Beach, stepping out for over an hour along the sand, meeting regulars, watching dogs.

'But I didn't swim much,' he says, and falls silent.

We watch the birds. The crows—or ravens—are glossy black gargoyles against the high blue sky and orange roof tiles. Their calls sound lonely. 'Ravens mate for life, you know, honey.'

I didn't know.

A magpie wheels in, landing under a rosebush, and immediately nabs a worm. Honeyeaters flit from sweetness to sweetness. I peel off my scarf.

'I never thought I'd live to see us locked away from each other,' Dad says after a while. 'I never could have imagined they'd stop us seeing our families.'

What I hear is that he was worried he might have died before we could get to him. I blink, telling him the sun is more intense here. He agrees it has been a hot summer. 'I couldn't even go out for Christmas.'

Another silence. The light so white. The day still.

'It's nearly lunchtime,' he tells me, so we return to his room. I must leave at noon—Covid visiting hours don't allow family members to stay for meals. We hold hands.

'I'll see you tomorrow,' I say. 'Amanda is coming this afternoon.'

'I'm so lucky,' he says. 'How long can you stay?'

'Three weeks,' I say.

'Wow!'

He kisses my hand. *HOPE* glimmers.

'Bye, Dad, see you tomorrow, bye, enjoy lunch, bye now, love you, bye, eat up, bye, love you . . .' So many words as I cross the four metres of his room. So many glimpses back. I close the door and wait on the other side, listening to his laboured breathing. I could reopen the door, to remind myself he's real, but I can hear him, just there, working to breathe. 'Ah. Ah. Ah . . .'

Next day, we have a family lunch at quarantine HQ. Amanda, Alanna and I shop for Dad's favourites—prawns and salmon, sparkling wine, thick bread, butter and cheeses. Judy has collected him and they arrive in high spirits. He is on his wheelie-walker but looks handsome in cream trousers and a freshly pressed shirt. It's white cotton with small navy palm trees on it, which I mistake for dragonflies, and he says I might need glasses more than him. He's curious about Airbnb, Brett's upcoming house build and Justin's son's driving lessons. He is on song. He even navigates the stairs and the long hallway to the bathroom, and then takes himself out into the warm afternoon for a smoke with Judy.

I watch them, puffing away together in the heat, laughing and teasing. It doesn't seem real that I can see him. He's so tiny, but he's himself: cheerful, grateful, wayward—and stubborn, too. When they return, he shows me his navy-and-white-striped socks and says the captain is still at the helm. Judy kisses him, saying yep, she still is.

Amanda, Alanna and I have a Zoom Art Day with our friend Louise in Melbourne. I borrow pencil and paper from Justin's son, an accomplished sketcher of birds and cars, to copy a Matisse drawing I'd seen before lockdown. When I visit Dad, I give it to him, and he applauds. Later, after showing the drawing to carer Miriam, he tells her about the time he had to shear a property's entire herd of sheep because the contractors didn't arrive. She says her grandmother was the only female shearer in WA, back in the day. 'You might have known her.'

'If I did, I'd remember her,' Dad says. 'Hell, I'd have asked her to marry me!'

We apply ourselves to the newspaper's nine-letter word. I'm trying to solve it on a piece of notepaper when Dad, who's sitting on his Brett-bought recliner chair, looks up. 'Wonderful,' he says.

I assume, for a moment, that he's commenting again on my burgeoning artistic talent, but then realise he has mulled his way to the solution.

'Amazing, Dad,' I say.

'Not really, honey. You just need to think quietly, without stressing.'

When I leave, I carry that thought. I wish I could imprint it on myself. I'm still frightened about the aneurysm that travelled with me across the country, terrified it will take me as that blood vessel took Peter. I remain fearful about Dad. His breathing is dire, yet he will take himself out under the trees to smoke. His ciggies are tucked into the top compartment of the walker.

I go to the beach for fish and chips with Sonia and Les. They are as solid in my life as parents or siblings or Pete. They ask after Dad, and I tell them how he insists that he's not getting old—he's just maturing.

I wonder if we ever will, Sonia says, and we laugh.

I would like to *grow* old, not just *get* old—and I'd like to do it around them. When we're together, everything feels easy, just as it did when Sonia and I slept head to toe as kids. No stressing with them. No aching head. No worries.

We raise our glasses—*To growing old*—as a molten sun drops into the darkening Indian Ocean.

A ROUTINE DEVELOPS. Each morning at Port Beach, where metal cranes like giant giraffes stand sentinel, I walk barefoot, out and back, along three kilometres of immaculate white sand. Then I plunge into the water. There's not much fish life, and no seahorses, but the colour is the aqua of childhood drawings—of Lucien Henry's vase in the waratah painting. It's sharper and fizzier than the harbour. Wake up, it shouts. Feel.

And we do. Sonia and I run squealing into the salt, watched over by our other old friend, Janet. Sonia does a tea-bag bob while I stroke parallel to the shore. Someone was taken by a shark only a few months ago, but how to resist this life-giving liquid? I'd forgotten how transparent everything is here—how exposed and exposing. I float above bleached stones (or bones), then fling myself under the shower. Why, I ask my chums, are outdoor ablutions so damn fine?

In the last photo Peter snapped of me, I'm naked, sheltered from view by tea-tree bushes, looking at him with delighted eyes. Droplets of water splash off my skin; hair swishes down my back. It was taken the day before his last birthday. I'd rented a shack on the south coast of Victoria, not far from his childhood lighthouse. We'd returned from the Southern Ocean, euphoric, and he clicked the pic.

Gotcha.

In Perth, the daily sluice kicks me into work: nesting for Dad. I search for lamps—those ones that don't have a switch, needing only the touch of a hand. I scour the city for a quilt cover, one that will work with his navy-blue recliner chair and oatmeal curtains. I track down a system that will allow us to hang paintings at different levels from the old-fashioned picture rails. No nails in his new digs.

While rain buckets relentlessly in Sydney, Perth is desert-dry. At Dad's unit, I water and deadhead his roses, then apply fertiliser. I collect mementoes to arrange on the side table in his room, telling him how I do it at home, and call them still lifes. He is intrigued by the plural. Shouldn't it be lives? No, because a *still life* is one singular object you see, and . . .

Words are fun; something we share.

Sometimes we talk about the book he wrote for us. A few years back, he mastered word processing and typed an account of his life, giving copies to his children for Christmas. It was called *Many Are the Memories*. He says he could add a whole chapter now. He asks about the book Mum wrote. Hers was called *My Bush Days*.

'That was where we were all happiest,' he says. 'Out there.'

He has a visit from a colleague who worked with him in real estate, after he left the factory. She tells me he had a reputation for honesty, refusing to quote high to get a listing, and advising people not to sell if the market was down. Frustratingly, he'd even suggest they use another agent sometimes. I'm reminded of Nick and his above-and-beyond care.

You have no idea who you are, do you?

I meet with the agent for Dad's unit and ask if I will need to have it painted. 'Nah. It will be renovated. Cosmetics aren't a factor,' he says bluntly.

They say that as we age and eyesight fades, we don't notice dust accumulating in our homes. Maybe we need others to see it for us. Did I let Dad down by not insisting on replacing the curtains? He was always so adamant, but now I see that parts of them are shredded. Have I done enough? Can I ever?

Still, it's good to be here. I know who I am. I'm a daughter, and I'm useful.

Brett and Justin have already done a major clear-out, taking away loads of linen and pots and pans, smaller pieces of furniture, books, CDs and DVDs, so Amanda and I begin the process of trying to sell or give away the major items of furniture. Auction houses tell us no one will buy 'brown stuff'; everyone prefers Swedish modern. I remember this from when

I was clearing our home—that tallboy that belonged to Peter's aunt—and I recall how the milk jug carries history when I look at Dad's dining chairs with the tulips carved into their backs. He can't fathom that no one would want them, or the big old table, and I understand. After Peter's death I took it as a personal rejection when treasures were seen as trash, even though I shed ruthlessly.

First to go was that still life with the dictionary.

The apple core went, into the rubbish with the avocado skins he'd composted the previous day, but his books were his life. His history. What to do with them?

The easy-to-read-use-and-understand French grammar went to his friend Rob—they shared a passion for the Geelong Football Club and all things Gallic. He tells me he still refers to it.

That began the process of gifting his library. I see now that it was a strategy to keep him alive. Conversely, it was also a ritual that helped me to comprehend he was gone. I would pore over his shelves before selecting appropriate books, then dedicate and deliver them, hoping they would be cherished by their new custodians.

His tattered, cloth-bound Shakespeare, with its yellowing bookmarks and newspaper clippings about the Bard, was wrapped in tissue and packed. How was I to let it go when it fell open at Sonnet 104?

To me, fair friend, you never can be old . . .

His dictionary was always going to be a keeper. On page after page, in the most surprising places, were those comments and connections. It was an alphabetical window into that curious, whimsical mind, and I consulted it daily. When I found a marking in Peter's hand, it was mostly a good surprise, but occasionally it bit . . .

De Stijl

Why had he had given that art movement two brackets and three ticks? Did he have interests I didn't know about? And if this was a secret, were there others? What if he had tried to tell me about this, and I'd been too busy to listen?

At Dad's unit, I'm surrounded by objects that hold stories I don't know: a velvet box of old coins, and teaspoons from places he visited, with landscape plaques for handles.

Keep? Or throw?

I take Grandpa's war medals to Dad, and as I'm deciding where to put them, he asks me to repeat something for a second time. I inquire which is his bad ear. He tells me it's the left, which is a good thing, because when he returns to driving, he won't be able to hear the backseat driver. Is that a hint?

There's a dinner set he bought at the beginning of his second marriage. He mentions this to all of us, and we realise it represents something important. Perhaps he and my stepmother had dreamed of being the kind of people who entertained at a table for twelve; people who made martinis, perhaps, or cooked beef Wellington. I'm not sure, but it was the sixties and the dinner set must have been an enormous outlay. Dad fixates on it until we promise Justin will keep it. It's the only time we wonder about Dad's mental faculties, but once we've assured him it's safe, he relaxes.

And then there are the bears. He has three—souvenirs from outings with Judy. He nods as I arrange them near her photo. The place is beginning to feel like a nest.

Amanda comes to the unit when she's not working remotely. We sweep and scrub as Sonia mows Dad's tiny lawn. Then we return to her place to watch footy, dancing in front of the TV when my Swans win. Les makes apple pies for us, and for Dad. I stay with them for a time, then move to a rented place. But that comes later . . .

I play Bananagrams with Dad, sipping wine and eating cheese in autumn sunshine. I buy a bar fridge so he can store wine, and Amanda installs it. I meet Campbell, the chaplain, who will become a stalwart. He's completing a PhD about a Frenchwoman who was held for decades as a prisoner of conscience. Dad says he won't be converted, and Chaplain Campbell says he wouldn't try. They swap stories about small towns and farms.

I fetch bowls for 'nibblies', so Dad can entertain Martin, who can no longer live alone after a stroke, and Bob, whose wife is in the dementia wing. I find Bob's humour abrasive.

'Cut him some slack, darling,' Dad says. 'It's a terrible scenario.'

Dad cuts a lot of slack, but he's not without a temper. It rears up when he fumbles the mobile phone, and his fuse shortens when he gets nicotine withdrawals. Still, he's chipper about Judy's upcoming birthday, and even talks about going out for a drink.

We have eight days of optimism, and then, on day nine, a Friday, Amanda and I arrive to find a sign saying the facility will be closed until further notice. Covid has landed.

We call Dad from the Falcon, parked just across the road. He is philosophical. 'What can we expect, darlings?' he says. 'As soon as they opened the state it was going to get in.' (I feel like a starling that should have been shot at the border.) Everybody is doing their best. We are not to worry about him. Everything will be fine, he repeats.

We call Brett and Justin and Judy. All of them make stinging one-word responses. We let Alanna know, because she was planning to visit. Then we drive to a shopping centre to fill the hours until we learn what 'further notice' means. We buy a gift for Dad to give Judy—a soft cream throw rug. We circle fluoro-lit corridors and ride elevators, finally settling on a quilt for Dad's bed. We track down photo frames but turn up our noses at artificial flowers. We still don't grasp what's ahead. Time moves in minute steps.

(*Minute* and *minute*, Pete—another English oddity.)

We're in a coffee shop, arranging for Dad to have a daily newspaper delivery, when we get an update on his only brother. He'd had a fall a few days earlier, and Justin reports that the outlook is now grim. The dark feathery thing is spreading its wings. I want to redirect its gaze away from me and mine.

Eventually, we hear that Dad is in lockdown. He may not leave his room, not even to go into the courtyard. All staff and residents will be PCR-tested, and the results will determine their days. But for now, we are locked out. He is locked in.

Give me a deity to murder. Give me ten of them.

We make a care package of edible treats and books of puzzles. We write long, loving notes to him, trying to be upbeat, and drive back to the facility where there are now signs forbidding entry. A nurse in full PPE gear comes to the door when we ring. Yes, she will deliver Dad's parcel, but it might take hours. They're understaffed before they even begin.

I wish I had binoculars to see the future. I wish I could speed clocks.

Or maybe I don't.

I drop Amanda back at the place we've just moved to. We hug forlornly, trying to reassure each other, and I head to Sonia's. Her mum is now locked down, too. We're pouring wine, reminding each other our parents are in good hands, when my phone rings. Dad's brother has died.

Feathers and fates and fury and sorrow, and oh, how do we tell him, alone in his anonymous room, with Covid trying to sink its talons into him? I sit on Les and Sonia's lawn, bare legs prickling, to call Amanda. We're both due to head home in three days, and it's unlikely we will be able to visit Dad without an exemption.

I feel a kind of vertigo. My unruly head tingles and throbs. I'm frightened the aneurysm is growing, or the neuralgia is returning, but I tell myself this is panic, this is not falling from thirty-five storeys. Amanda's voice is as steady as ever, and I calm, deciding there and then, under Les's spreading eucalypt, that I will cancel my flight and stay. We'll request an exemption for Amanda to visit Dad tomorrow, so she can see him before she leaves, and break the news about his brother's death.

We hang up. I drag myself inside, where Brett and Justin have arrived, along with Sonia's brothers and Janet. We raise glasses—Dad would want it. Not long after, we're joined by two old friends whose father, a man I've known since my late teens, died only a few hours ago. Someone should take a lottery ticket.

We take turns patting Brett's sweet-natured dog, insisting to each other that things have a way of working out. For three hours, around Sonia's table, it seems they might. But the image of our frail father, behind a closed door in that unfinished, utilitarian room, not knowing that things will get so much worse, haunts me all night.

Lockdown. Iso. Quarantine. Tick. Tick. Tick.

Next morning, after being briefed about the facility's outbreak management plan, Amanda is kitted up in visor and overalls and taken to meet Dad in the courtyard, where, under the ravens' eyes, she tells him his brother has died. I wait to hear how he has taken it. Stoic, of course, Amanda reports. Quiet.

'Ah . . .'

When I call, he keeps repeating that he is the sick one; he has emphysema and heart problems. His brother was the young one (my uncle was ninety) and it isn't right, it isn't how it should be. And siblings are the witnesses of our lives, he says. They know us like no one else. He says to remember that, because once they are gone . . .

I tell him to conserve energy because he may have Covid, then realise how stupid that is. Grief will have its way.

Amanda and I drop off another care package, and this time we include half-a-dozen old photos. After a few hours, we call him. We sit in his car, at his favourite beach, asking for the stories behind the pictures. It's a personal retrospective. We record his voice as he speaks of his mother, his cousins, his childhood, his brother.

When we're informed he has tested positive, it's no surprise. How could they possibly keep it contained? There is no anger or blame, just a sense of the inevitable, and a tsunami of anxiety as I imagine Covid hanging over him, like a peregrine about to drop.

Amanda leaves. I miss her immediately, and sleep flies away with her.

Afterwards, I move to another rental, my fourth digs in three weeks. There was the house with Alanna and Amanda, then Sonia's, then the place with Amanda, and now this haven with mosaic paths underfoot, magpies and willie wagtails harmonising, and a black cocker spaniel called Pearl. I unpack and lie down. My heart beats in my head.

In the days that follow, I deliver packages of lemon drink, lottery tickets and old photos. I include letters full of questions, and over the phone I'm given yarns in return; snippets of long ago.

'There aren't many photos from when I was little,' he says, 'because it was so expensive to get a picture taken.'

Now I understand why he keeps all his old cameras. I remember that framed photo in my flat—the snowy-haired cherub in rompers. His parents probably saved for months to document their firstborn.

There are two miniscule black-and-white snaps of their house—Dad has no idea who might have taken them—with a bullock wagon out front. The place was little more than a one-room lean-to in the middle of nowhere, but Dad tells stories of playing knucklebones and helping Grandpa with chores, of leaving a secure job at the bank to go jackarooing, and of his collie dog Rick and the many sheep he could hold in a moving mob. He talks at snail's pace, his breathing laboured, but he keeps going, like a pilgrim walking a long trail.

These telephone monologues—him in solitary with the *aaark* of crows from his courtyard and me by the beach under the bickering of gulls, phones pressed to our ears to get every word—are gifts for me and, hopefully, diversion for him in his grief . . . along with the nine-letter word puzzle, of course.

'It's called Target, darling,' he says, 'and I usually hit it.'

Days pass. I swim, lying in the salt and looking up into the sky of my childhood. I try to describe to Dad how everywhere that is not here looks faded. He asks me if there are clouds on the horizon, and I say there is one, in the distance.

'What do you think it weighs?' he asks, and I admit to never having considered the weight of a cloud. I ask him to hang on while I google, and find an article that says a single cumulus cloud weighs the same as 100 elephants.

'Wow!' he says, then coughs, and I'm unsure if I've helped or made things worse.

I water his roses in hopes of a bud, then prepare a new batch of photos and drop them to the nurse, who looks exhausted behind her fogged mask and glasses. Back at my digs, I work, tapping at my keyboard like a falcon chick pipping at a shell, and then I phone for my dose of memories. Dad's seahorses are still active, but he is weakening and can't talk for long.

'Sorry, honey,' he says. 'Sorry.'

The thought of the virus in Dad's fragile lungs sends me into a mania of activity. At his unit, I fill bins and arrange for rubbish collections. I'm struck by how anonymous the rooms look; how forlorn. It's like he never lived there.

A young woman buys Dad's sideboard. Her father secures it on his truck, and I give them the pillows from Dad's sagging sofa to protect it. She's moving into her first home.

'I like old things,' she says. 'I like the smell of the wood, and I think about all the people that polished it. Old stuff has stories.'

Sonia is with me, but I can't look at her. I know she will be near tears. I want to hug this child guru, but instead I ask if she is studying.

'Nah, I'm a carer,' she says. 'I work with old people and disabilities.'

Then we do cry.

We stand in the driveway, waving, telling each other the world is good. It really is. Imagine if that young woman were caring for our parents, we say. Well, that's what most carers are like, we remind each other. The world is kind. Good. Kind.

Do we protest too much?

Later, the young carer sends a photo of herself with the sideboard. She writes that she is *sure that would have been hard to part with. I'll look after it, I promise.*

A couple come for Dad's wooden tulip chairs and the heavy dining table. Nadia is delighted with everything, and besotted with Jim. They're getting married—*second time around for both of us*—and want Dad's furniture for the wedding.

When we upturn the table, we discover crayon drawings on the underside. They must have been made more than forty years ago, when Justin and Amanda were tots.

All this, I get to tell Dad because he does survive Covid.

He lives. Oh! He lives.

We're informed that one person will be allowed to visit him for a single hour each day. My brothers and Judy insist that I take the daily slot. I will see him on Sunday, two days hence.

I move into my fifth home in as many weeks. Now I know how Dad felt when he was being shunted from bed to bed, from hospital to respite. It's like when we were kids going from Mum's house to Dad's place, to Mum's next place to our grandmother's. It isn't bad. But it doesn't allow for much relaxation.

My hypervigilance is exacerbated by unfamiliar paths to bathrooms, low ceiling beams and uneven steps. Both sides of my head throb in the night, but that doesn't matter. Dad has lived, after sixteen long days with no eye-to-eye contact other than brief carer visits with food and medicines. My forty-seven-kilo father has defied the predator, without complaining—except on the days when his paper was late. Then we all heard about it.

A nine-letter word comes to mind . . .

acclimate
adapt physiologically to environmental stress

Like the falcons and the seahorses, Dad adapted. He may not have thrived, but he has survived.

IT'S THE FINAL Sunday in March and at last I'm to visit Dad for my allotted hour. I'm awake before the sun rises so I creep out, trying not to disturb my landlady. My legs find their rhythm and I head over to Dad's unit to water before the heat of the day. There's a bud on his favourite rose. I harvest it for him. A sign. I find a two-dollar coin on the pavement—another sign—and decide I'm meant to buy him a scratchie.

After Peter died, I was sent an article titled 'Ten Signs to Watch Out For From Deceased Loved Ones', and yes, I did read it, even though I loathed the word *deceased* almost as much as *passed*. Passed what? Passed who? He didn't pass. He died. It's a perfectly good verb. He died.

Or maybe he didn't . . .

The writer of the article believed I was walking through a crowd of restless 'loved ones' who were dropping hints everywhere like hankies. How? Well, lights flicking on and off were indications that 'spirit is present'. An insect or bird meant the loved one was not alone. A high-frequency buzzing in the ears was a call to be alert for a message. At night, the buzzing never let up, but it was a fight/flight adrenaline response, according to my GP. After months of resistance to sleeping tablets, she told me to go home and have a glass of wine.

'Let go,' she said. 'You can't control anything, so stop trying. Just one glass.' That remedy would have appealed to Dad.

The writer also insisted that an object in the path carried a message. I scoffed. What was the message? Sweep the paths?

Yet as I walk uphill from Dad's unit to buy his lottery ticket, I tell myself that maybe this coin is a sign. I don't believe it's from the afterlife, but perhaps things are on the up for Dad now. The man who calls himself lucky is due for a win.

Outside the front door of the nursing home, I take my obligatory Covid test and have my temperature taken. In the foyer, a noticeboard greets me. On it are eight photographs—smiling faces I'd seen sixteen days ago. There's the man whose wife would visit every evening to feed him dinner. There's the woman who would sing to the caged budgerigars, and the one who always wore hot pink. In the week before Covid swooped, I'd come to know most of the faces on that board, even if only to wave, and now they're gone; statistics in a health report.

I continue along the corridor, noting furniture stacked against walls and sealed-off doors. Staff in protective gear duck their heads and scurry past. At Dad's door, I knock.

'That you, honey?'

'Sure is.'

'Come on in, then.'

He lies, prone, on rumpled white sheets, wearing short navy-blue pyjama pants and a long-sleeved green top. I am aghast at how thin he is. I hadn't thought it possible he had weight to lose.

'Hel-lo,' he half-sings, making no effort to sit up or move, which tells me all I need to know. My father always stands; always moves to greet, to offer a chair. Now there is just his open mouth and an unfocused stare. I wasn't ready for this. I've been in the land of dropped coins and feathery fortunes. He asks how I am, and as I tell him, I take stock.

His exposed calves, thinner than my arms, are covered by a catastrophe of blood blotches. A large white bandage is stuck to his right leg, just below the knee, blood seeping through it. The dun-coloured carpet is a patchwork of red stains from where his feet have bled as he has made his way to the bathroom. His nose is blood-encrusted. His fingers and the backs of his hands are mottled with blood, and it cakes under his fingernails. His skin is grey, a colour fit for the wing of a tern but not for Dad's face.

His gaze worries me most. He just stares at the ceiling. The winged thing has not taken him, but it's as though he knows it is hovering and he must scan for danger. He smiles when I say how proud I am that he kicked the virus, but his eyes flicker away, upwards. I'm masked so can't kiss him, but we hold hands awhile in silence.

'Look, Dad,' I say eventually, retrieving the rosebud. 'It's from home.'

'Ahhhh . . .' He manages a sound, but his breathing is laboured so I don't offer it to him to smell. I locate a vase and place it on his bedside table. That's when I notice the room's new inhabitant. It's an oxygen machine, with a long plastic breathing tube and two prongs that can be inserted into his nose. He tells me he doesn't use it much but has needed it in the last couple of days.

'But not often,' he says again, as though it's an indulgence, like wine or chocolate.

The floor is a mess of bloody tissues, cardboard food utensils and paper cups. During lockdown, all meals have had to be delivered on disposable plates with disposable cutlery, he tells me. Another day, I will observe him trying to cut his food and will see how hopeless the soft wooden fork is for someone so weak. He can't keep the plate in place; the knife isn't sharp enough. He gives up, this man who could once slaughter a sheep.

I bustle, determined not to cry. I find food I'd delivered and check use-by dates. He has barely touched anything. I clean his refrigerator, then use bath towels to dust every surface. I stack photos and notes and cards, arrange fallen teddy bears and hang clothing. He watches, eyes still flickering upwards, and when the room is clearer, and his newspapers are piled by the door for collection, I ask if there's anything he'd like. No, he says. He's fine.

He isn't.

I ask about the bleeding, and he shakes his head, turning away from me. I wait. Eventually, he rolls back and says he can't stop it; they can't stop it. He gasps for air, then manages to say he is embarrassed about it.

'I'm so ashamed,' he says.

'Why, Dad?' I try not to let my distress show. 'Why? You've got emphysema and you're on thinners for your heart, but you kicked Covid to the kerb. There should be a parade. It's a bloody miracle.'

'Don't say *bloody*,' he says, managing a smile.

'You're incredible,' I say. 'And we will get it sorted.'

'No,' he speaks loudly, making his breath catch. 'This is like nothing I've ever had before. I can't make myself tidy. And you be careful, honey, or you'll catch the bloody thing.'

I'm reminded of a friend who was dying of AIDS, decades ago, and how he screamed at me in terror one day when I was cleaning up.

'Don't touch my shit. You'll die.'

Blood. Shit. Shame. Bodies as enemies. Fluids as foe. Vomit on sheets. Dry crust on a nose. Patches on the back of a dress . . .

My first ever date was with a boy whose father was an architect, charming and smooth, and whose mother served 'high teas'. I met the boy at uni. His brothers also studied there, following a tradition established by his grandfather and great-uncles. The boy was amazed that I was the first in my clan to study past high school. Thanks to the short-lived Labor government, I could sprawl for free on those green lawns, and I too could posture in tutorials.

We had been out to a Sunday session at the uni pub, and afterwards he pulled his smart cherry-red car off the highway into Mum's drive. He made no comment on the traffic volume or noise—impeccable manners—and I decided that it had all gone the way it was meant to. We said our goodbyes, and before he could come to my door, I swung it open, twirled around to close it, thanked him and waved, my floral skirt swishing, my sandaled feet skipping up the stairs and inside—only to discover that I had got my period on the drive home and there was a great slash of brownish blood on the fabric, which meant it would be on his white sheepskin seat cover and he, or his coiffed mother, would have to clean it. Romance was slain. Mortification. Seeping from me . . .

I never heard from him again and I was too ashamed to call to apologise, so I can't make light of Dad's feelings. I just wait, holding his hand. He's a hero—a starved survivor of a war waged on his insides while he was weak from grief for his brother. I gently wipe every bit of blood from his body, and then take his sorbolene cream and rub it into his hands, up his arms and across his poor tired face.

'Ah,' he says, over and over. 'Ah . . .'

I lift his lightweight left leg and place his foot on the bed's rail. I rub cream onto his toes that are so like mine, and onto his heel and sole, wishing I could massage consolation into his soul. I apply cream all the way up his calves and thighs, carefully, so carefully, for fear of breaking his skin. No more blood. Please, no more.

There are splotches behind his knees and on the base of his feet, but while they are elevated, there's no bleeding. I keep rubbing, and he drifts, eyes closing and opening. I've been with him for well over an hour, but no one comes to chase me away, so I just keep applying cream. Skin to skin. Daughter to father. Silence broken only by his breath and his elongated vowel sounds.

Ahhhh. Ohhhh. Ahhhh.

I stay almost three hours. Carers come and go, but they don't tell me to leave. Eventually, though, I ask how he is going and he says he will sleep. I pull up the bloodstained sheet, then his quilt, and tuck him in. It's warm outside, but he's chilly.

'Not much coverage on me,' he says. 'Can't fatten a thoroughbred.'

I repeat that we're all proud of him, and he shakes his head. I didn't do anything, he says. The nurses did it all. He says he still can't believe his brother went before him, and I wonder if that's why he is looking up—maybe he's picturing my uncle, somewhere just out of view. I tell him how sorry I am. How sorry we all are. I remind him the funeral is in four days, and that Brett and Justin will attend, while I will be with him. I say we can watch online, if he wants that, but he just shakes his head and closes his eyes. I've rarely seen Dad cry, and I'm not sure if he will now, but he holds a hand over his eyes until his breathing settles.

I am gathering up my things when he asks me how long I'm staying.

'Haven't you already been here for a few weeks?'

'Yep. Twenty-seven days now, Dad. But who's counting?'

'You'll need to be getting home,' he says.

'Nah. They've had torrential rain every day I've been here,' I say. 'I'm much better where it's sunny. Always the opportunist, me, you know that.'

He shakes his head, then reaches for my hand, holding on to it with his bent fingers. My skin pulses with life, while his is thin and blood-blotched, but my bracelet insists on hope.

'Thank you for coming, darling,' he says. As though I've done him some great favour. 'Sorry I'm not better company.'

That bloody word.

After Peter died, apologising became a reflex. I said sorry to him incessantly (wherever he was) for not being with him at the end. I said it to everyone. I even apologised in dreams. One day, I bumped into Alanna, who was loading the dishwasher.

'Sorry,' I said.

'That's the fourth time you've apologised in the last half-hour,' she said.

'Sorry,' I said immediately, and then, when she spun around: 'I know. I'm sorry.'

When I apologised to the crockery cupboard for slamming its door, we both collapsed into laughter. I remember the strangeness of the sound, and the guilt at finding anything amusing.

Now, I want to ban Dad from saying sorry, but he's fading, so I tiptoe to the door, looking back over my shoulder, checking he really is there, really breathing, really alive.

I will stay eight weeks and sleep in eight different beds. I get skilled at packing, and my massage technique improves. Dad is constantly itchy, so I rub cream onto his back and chest, and after the first few times, I don't even flinch at how skeletal he is. I cut his fingernails and toenails, amazed at how they grow long and strong, when everything else is shrinking. His hair sprouts too, and a hairdresser comes to give him a trim. He sits up straight when she tells him he's handsome. He manages to eat a little and strengthens incrementally. On one red-letter day, he ventures into the courtyard. Ravens chorus as we sip wine—'just a snifter'—and he thrashes me at Bananagrams. I'm outraged but also euphoric. He talks about having a cigarette as a reward.

He dresses in structured clothes again and starts to look like a starved version of his old self, but he still won't leave the nursing home. I suppose it is fear of Covid, as well as exhaustion. Not even a ride in his Falcon can tempt him out. I ache to drive him to Port Beach; to sit in the warm car looking into the blue of the offing. I want him to see a horizon again. But he says he's content so I must accept that.

One day, I knock on his door as usual.

'Come in, darling,' he calls.

'Darling' walks in to find Dad perched on the edge of his bed, spindly legs dangling. On the rocker, sits a man-mountain wearing a camouflage uniform of black and grey.

'It's the navy,' Dad says, as though a fleet has been dispatched. 'They're here to help, aren't you, Will?'

'Yep, here to help, sir.'

Will stands then, and both Dad and I make the same involuntary backward tilt, as if to resist being sucked towards him, like filings to a magnet.

'Excellent to talk,' Will says. 'I'll be back later to look at that aircon.' He takes Dad's fingers into his great paw and gently, so gently, shakes.

'Good, Will. Yes. Later,' Dad echoes. I sit on the navy chair, while Dad talks of his new friend's frigate and the crew and the wide, wine-dark sea. It's the ocean I swim in each morning, but somehow it seems different when I imagine a crew of Wills on it.

This visit will intrigue Dad for days, but ultimately it will be tiny Jenn, receptionist and bringer of good cheer, who will fix the aircon.

I hand over the keys to the real estate agent on the same day I collect the keys for my sixth short-term rental. I take a bottle of sparkling wine to Dad, wanting to mark this ending consciously, rather than pretending it hasn't happened, but he wearies quickly. How much more must he let go?

Les makes Dad a compilation CD of all his favourites and 'What a Wonderful World' is on high rotation until the bleeding recurs. Dad makes the decision to go off his thinners, despite the risk to his heart.

After his carpet is shampooed, and the evidence of his 'crime' has been erased, I tell him about the man who made our house pristine after Peter's death. He remarks that you'd be surprised what people leave behind when they vacate houses. I've never before considered that both my parents had to deal with the detritus of other people's pasts.

Reading aloud from the paper to Dad, I come across the name of a coastal town I used to visit as a teenager.

'Yallingup,' I say. 'It's a great-sounding word, isn't it?'

'Dwellingup's better,' he says.

'I like Cowaramup,' I say.

'Cunderdin, Kondinin and Boyanup,' he recites, wheezing.

'Koolyanobbing,' I say, trumping him.

He breathes for a while, the oxygen machine thumping away beside him. Maybe the game has been too much. Then . . .

'Wilyabrup,' he whispers.

Neither of us mentions Yalgoo. It's where Mum and my step-father lived, after they sold the farm. Neither do I mention that, before I left Sydney, I found the original decree nisi from Mum and Dad's divorce. Sometimes silence is the kindest thing, and we're good at it now. We sit, saying nothing, for ages. I hold his hand as he closes his eyes.

One morning, the ocean is palest blue-green. Gliding through the brine at sunrise, it's as though my seahorses wake and I remember the bottles Mum would unearth near old mining camps or abandoned stone houses. Common, they were. Not collectible. But they were the colour of this ocean I'm swimming in now.

The water glimmers like millions of glass filings, its waves crisp-edged as they furl onto the hard-packed sand. I picture Dad as he once was, his skinny legs bounding along this beach.

Memories live in this place. My own memories. They rise and rise.

It's like I've always been here, and I wonder if perhaps I should stay indefinitely. I have purpose here; worth. I have this tiny man who allows me to care for him, and he is getting stronger as the room fills with familiars. In addition to objects he loves and remembers, other visitors are allowed now, and he lights up when the brothers and Judy can come.

Justin and his tall basketballer sons construct a flat-pack desk, and Dad enjoys watching for the first half-hour, but then lies down. He has never seen an Ikea set-up before. Justin remarks that it's more complicated than the house Brett's building, and as the four of them laugh, their shared bloodline is obvious.

I relax. I even sleep. I walk, swim, write, do an occasional and very welcome voice job, run errands and sit with Dad. I adapt. It's as though Sydney, with its daily La Niña deluges, is just a place on the news. The three-hour time difference reduces to two as autumn settles in, and it becomes easier to communicate with my clan on the east coast. Alanna jokes—but it's only a half-joke—that maybe I'm going to move back to Perth. After all, it's where we were nestlings. Sonia and I agree how lovely it is to be in each other's daily lives for the first time in forty years. We have coffee with Janet at the beach and reminisce. We know all about each other. Well, the early all. Sometimes I wonder if that's the most important stuff.

And I notice another thing. I feel safe around Dad. I don't know whether it's because I'm too focused on his needs to fret about my own, or whether there is some vestige of childhood that tells me nothing bad can happen if I'm with him, but the cause is immaterial. The lived experience is relief. There is some peace, dropping slow.

But I do have medical tests to take, and there's the life I've been forging—personal and professional—since Peter died. There's my flat, abandoned for eight weeks, even though my neighbours are caring for it. It's time. Dad is stabilising. His room is warm and inviting, and while he enjoys my daily visits, we both know I'm not needed as I was. He wants to feel ordinary again. So I will go.

On my final morning, after I swim, I watch an osprey hanging in mid-air. Perhaps it has seen a rat in the saltbush and is keeping watch, but it looks more like pure pleasure, suspended there, wings barely beating, supported by upward gusts. If our ancestors and beloveds, those we knew and those who came before, really do dissolve and dissipate, and if their cells really are all around us, then that bird is held there by Mum and Peter and Robin and my grandmother Molly and Ning and Grandpa and great-great-grandparents and billions of others of the long-dead. The osprey, on its updraft, is kept aloft by absences. Perhaps I am too.

I RISE TO a sodden Sydney morning. Bright flowers greet me, along with a fridge full of food. There's also a book, sitting on torn but exquisite paper. The looping scrawl on the nearby card belongs to the Elegant Backstroker. She'd got my key from Neighbour Fran and her gifts welcomed me when I arrived last night. I make tea, noting cobwebs and dust—but also the plants that have survived, tended for me while I've been tending Dad.

In a rain-break, I go down to my car, expecting the battery to be dead. Instead, I open the door to catastrophe. Every inch of the interior—carpets, steering wheel, dashboard, seats—is coated in thick white mould. The stench whacks me. I reel back, slam the door and step away.

While I've been in dry western heat, Sydney has had its wettest autumn in decades. Maybe ever. It's impossible to ignore the climate emergency when I look around the muddy garden.

Tectonic plates are shifting, and now it's not fire but water calling to us to act, and fast.

But first: this car.

Insurance won't cover it—there must have been a leaky seal—but experts agree it will be dangerous to drive because of the mould in the air system. A man offers to buy it for parts. He arrives wearing PPE gear like he's immersing himself in Covid. I watch him drive it away and feel nothing. It's a car, not a person. Six months ago, I might have gnashed my teeth, but not now. There's a bus stop out front and a ferry down the hill. My legs are strong.

A local friend leaves a gift—a bucket filled with mould killer, gloves, masks and a crimson hibiscus—and the work begins: tossing my beloved red patent-leather boots, now coated in fuzz; cleaning white spots from every black item in my wardrobe; and black spots from windowsills and doorframes.

Once again, I'm discarding. I picture Dad in his institutional room. If he can live with so little, then I can let go, too. Mum reduced her world to two suitcases. Peter's and mine was less than half a truck. Mould is only the beginning. I ransack cupboards. If I haven't used it for a year, out it goes. If I'm keeping it for an emergency, chuck it. I've seen emergencies, and stuff doesn't help.

I lighten with every bag that's tossed. I am making space, even if I don't know what it's for; I'm preparing for something, though I don't know when it will come: *the readiness is all . . .*

Days shorten. The harbour water is now warmer than the air. One evening, as I'm out walking with the determined but ever-more-frail Pilgrim, the bay bubbles and shakes, as though there's a squall moving across the surface.

'Mullet,' a local fisherman mutters.

Then we see them. The water is thick with a silvery swarm of fish, hundreds of them swimming together in a mass. At its edges, two seals patrol, their heads like those of black labradors, herding the fish toward the shore then out again, feasting. We humans stand, transfixed, as a massacre plays out.

Later, when I report to Dad, he whistles, saying how lucky I am to see that 'muster' on my doorstep. He goes on to tell me about his collie dog Rick, and I settle in for a story I've heard many times before. There can be pleasure in the old as well as the new.

I get excited—as I'm sure Peter would—about a local candidate for the federal election. I drop leaflets and wave signs at passing cars with other locals and am elated when she wins the seat. She's part of a political force called the Teals. The word reminds me of kookaburra wings, which may be apt, because climate is one of their main concerns. A new government is sworn in. Dad says *a little bird told him* I might be pleased with the outcome. We used to argue about politics, but in recent years we've inched closer to agreement—or tolerance, at least. Smiling is easier than scowling, Dad says.

Amanda flies to Perth. She sees Dad twice and he's frail but delighted. Then she gets Covid and has to spend a week in isolation. She can't visit Dad again before she must leave.

At the beginning of winter, as skies turn molten gold, I wing west. Dad is sleepier and thinner, but still of good cheer, and still a natural wordsmith.

'I may not be exhilarated, darling, but I'm not exhausted yet either,' he tells me one morning as he struggles with his trousers. They are clownish, the fabric swimming on his frame.

I plunge with Sonia and have dinners with her brothers and mine, but the days are all for Dad. One afternoon, while sitting in the courtyard, we hear music from the recreation room.

'They dance sometimes,' Dad tells me.

I ask if he'd like to go in to watch, but he demurs, telling me to duck my head in and take one of the 'oldies' for a spin.

When I open the sliding glass door, I'm met with a blast of Bing Crosby. Millie sashays with her walker and Betsy circles the room, sliding her feet and swaying her hips. There are no men tripping the light fantastic, and most of the women are seated, nodding or clapping, but their smiles are wide. I return to Dad and we talk about the pleasures of 'cutting a rug'. He and Judy always loved to dance, he says. I tell him about the village squares in Spain where people twirled spontaneously in warm night air.

'Did you?' he asks.

I did. Once, I wandered down an alley following the rhythms of cha-cha and chanced upon a group of men and women, slicked and primped, ballroom dancing in high style. I was invited onto the wooden floor, and it was only when one man asked if I'd like to come live there that I understood I'd entered the garden of a geriatric home.

'Wow,' Dad says. 'Bit different to here.'

'They sure could caper,' I tell him.

We sit a moment, both tapping along to Frank Sinatra. Eventually, Dad speaks. 'Caper is a funny word, isn't it?'

As we discuss the oddity of it being a dance and a heist and a small salty fruit, I'm caught by how much this conversation resembles those I had with Peter. These men of few words, who love words.

'Peter and I got together because I invited him to dance, you know.'

'No. I didn't, honey. You never told me.'

Mr Sinatra is asking to be flown to the moon, and Dad's eyes have closed, so I'm startled when he takes my hand in his.

'Let go of the grief, darling,' he says. 'It's no way to hang on to a person you love.'

I nod, keeping hold of his hand.

I get takeaway, one evening, and am given a fortune cookie.

Gratitude is not only the greatest of virtues, I read, *but the parent of all the others.*

I cry then, for my lucky grateful man, and when I rub my eyes I make things worse because there's chilli on my fingers. I google the quote, expecting it to have come from Confucius or Lao-Tzu. Instead, I find it's from that well-known Chinese philosopher and statesman, Cicero!

A few days later, Dad falls, and I'm immediately on alert, but he insists it was 'only a slide to the floor, darling'. I can't believe he has not smashed bones. There is nothing covering them but skin and fabric. I'm so afraid for him—it was a fall that began his decline—but he rallies, and before I leave completes half a lap of the corridors on his wheelie-chair.

Back in wintry Sydney, I take to dipping in the middle of the day as a reward after five hours at the desk. One sunny after-noon, I spy what might be a dark stingray in the shallows, but as I swim closer its 'tail' becomes one of eight legs—it's an octopus. Large, brown and knobbly, it marches away towards the deep, indignant at being stalked by a human.

'It was in a huff,' I tell Dad. 'But it was magnificent. It had white eyes.'

'Lucky you, honey,' he says, and I don't argue.

Later, I'm able to report to him that it also had a beak like a cockatoo, and that its botanical name is *Octopus tetricus*, which translates as 'gloomy octopus'.

I look up at the pinprick of the evening star, and hunt for a sliver of moon. I ferry to the city, and wander through the

Botanic Gardens, passing ibises with their prehistoric beaks and scalloped wings, to visit my waratah painting. It's still in situ, still like new. There are no age lines to weary it, and it has not faded. I've read somewhere, since my last visit, that staring into Islamic patterns is a kind of prayer.

The gallery is planning a revamp, I tell Dad later, and I'm concerned they won't rehang my picture.

'Well, nothing's permanent, darling,' he reminds me. I don't think he's talking about art.

Winter swims are choppy and frothy. Some days it's like being a sock in a washing machine, but as I gulp in water I'm glad of the icy reminder that I'm strong, bristling with life, and that the vessel in my brain is stable. I walk the shoreline, noting flotsam and jetsam—a glistening blood-red strawberry, shaped like a heart, at my feet; a dead flathead, eyeing me off; an apple core and dental flosser, to make me think of Peter.

Walking past a house down near the cove, I see a sign on the door.

No visitors. Don't knock. Not a good day. Thanks for thinking of Ted.

I can't stop thinking of Ted.

I watch the local pelican taking off. Its wings thwack-thwack-thwack the surface of the harbour as it heaves into the air. Rising is work.

A volcano erupts and the plague roils on. Eustasy, still. Some days it's as though the earth would like to throw off humans, like a dog ridding itself of fleas. But then, two dolphins arch their way across the cove, dark parentheses frolicking for me alone, and I feel welcomed and comforted.

Pay attention, they seem to be saying. *We're always here.*

I have a visit from an old friend, a paramedic. He is summoned out here, to the cliffs, often, but this is a social call so we have time to unpack more than the carry-on baggage of our days. I ask how he manages his internal life; whether dealing with suicide and death becomes ordinary. He says it never does, not for a second, but he does remark that he never feels lonelier than when he's performing CPR.

I ask if he can tell immediately if someone is dead, and he says no, but then describes being called out to a man who'd had a heart attack. The alarm was raised by the man's small son. On arrival, my friend knew the father had died, but he performed CPR for a long time because, he said, he wanted that little boy to be able to grow up without feeling that maybe he could have done something more to stop the great winged thing from taking his father. I want to hug him.

We talk about Peter, whom my friend loved, and he explains to me that traces of vomit often indicate a neurological crash. We discuss my aneurysm. He uses a term I've not heard before: 'thunderclap pain'. He says I should watch out for it—that Peter would probably have experienced it briefly. When I ask what

I should do if it occurs, he shakes his head and says we won't dwell on it.

He says Covid has been harder than he'd expected. No, not so much the mental health issues, or people wanting to end their lives, but the myriad new ways in which death can come. He tells me about a young schoolteacher, giving a remote lesson via Zoom to a class of littlies, who dropped dead onscreen. It took ages for someone to call an ambulance because the children thought she was playing hide-and-seek. Having no experience of death, they couldn't leap to the worst conclusion.

In July, Amanda and I return to the west for Dad's ninety-second birthday. 'I'm not getting old,' he repeats for us. 'I'm maturing.'

It's a low-key affair. He's still only allowed two visitors at a time, during limited hours. He's not up to leaving the facility, which deflates us because we had hoped to have afternoon tea at Justin's, so we each have separate visits with him to make the day more fun. In a sunny spot in the courtyard, I click a photo of him giving me his best Clint Eastwood stare.

'Go ahead,' he deadpans. 'Make my day.'

We raise glasses and drink bubbly in the winter light, and he belly laughs when I flash him, lowering my mask. I tell him I've done the sums, and that ninety-two years equals 34,815,744,000 seconds. I write it on a piece of paper, and he says he feels like Methuselah.

I stay ten days, and often the two of us just sit together in silence. Sometimes I read, and it's a familiar pleasure to ingest a story in quiet company. We play word games, of course. Anagrams remain his favourite, but we mix it up, trying to find words within words. *Paint* contains *pain*. *Hearth* contains *heart*. That one makes sense to us. It's like we're searching for hidden meanings, or maybe it's a way of saying the things that are uncomfortable or difficult. *Plover* contains both *love* and *over*, Dad comments one day, and I wonder what took him to that word. Did he begin with the bird? Or did he begin with *over*? Or *love*? He is triumphant when he tells me *endodontist* contains *dodo*. I want to tell him he's an old owl, that I enjoy his sideways wisdom, but I can't see how I can without being soppy, and that would not do.

Doubt creeps back in about where I should be. Real life is here in Perth; anywhere else would just be biding time. Leaving Dad is always hard, but now that his world is reducing, the thought of going is excruciating. Despite his constant refrain that he is 'fine', it's clear he's not. He barely eats and doesn't read the paper. My dream of him once again seeing a a wider patch of sky than the courtyard offers, is gone. Small mercies are all he wants, he insists. A visit. A phone call. Cashews.

'Those parmesan biscuits are good,' he says, so I buy five packets, hoping they will supplement the cornflakes which, he maintains, are all he wants for dinner. He fades, saying he's 'resting peacefully' whenever I arrive—meaning he is no longer getting out of bed. He sleeps and sleeps.

I don't know what to do or who to be. 'Daughter' is the only role that makes sense, but it also makes no sense to keep moving from Airbnb to Airbnb for the sake of a forty-minute visit each day. Dad insists I return to Sydney for my medical check-ups.

'Now I can say you need your head read and it's not an insult,' he says. We manage a little laugh about that.

I leave again. It's vile.

Back in Sydney, the follow-up MRI shows the aneurysm is stable. Marina has an exhibition of glowing floral still lifes. Peter's and my thirty-fifth wedding anniversary arrives, and I experience a wash of happiness. For a long time, all I felt was despair, fixating on the hard stuff because it was agony to picture him alone at the end with the thunderclap pain.

This anniversary, I recall adventures and silliness. I remember his life and not his solitary death. I invoke the living, instead of imagining the dying. I go out onto the balcony in the cold to look up at the canopy of stars, and I find one that could be him.

'Thanks, Pete,' I say.

I think about Dad and how he thanks everyone, every single carer and cleaner and offspring, for everything, and I see how both these men lived respectful lives of decency and kindness—that most undervalued of qualities. I wonder if I chose Peter because Dad was my template.

For years, it has felt to me like Peter went at a million miles an hour and never looked back. As irrational as I know it is, that hurt. But it occurs to me, standing on the balcony in shivery night air, that perhaps I never looked for him in the right places. I've always scanned my own memories, but they were overshadowed by grief. So, in the following days, I stop relying on my seahorses and look through photo albums and letters, and find so much I've forgotten. I revisit the stars and, maybe it's because it's winter, they seem closer, winking at me.

I go to Melbourne for a writers' festival, and make a personal pilgrimage, a peregrination, into the city and all the way to the falcons' building, into the foyer where Peter and I would watch. It looks bigger, and there's now a schmick cafe with a stylised abstract of a falcon above the bar. But over in the far corner, there is the screen, with a patient mother bird sitting on her eggs. I'm told there are four, like last year. I hope their outcomes will be better than Runty's.

I take tea with Peter's sister and niece—the maestra of minestrone—and I sip bubbles with Alanna and Amanda while we talk to Dad. He has never been able to master FaceTime. We tried it once, but all we saw was the hairy interior of his ear.

I watch my beloved Swans lose the grand final to Peter's old team, and I don't mind. The defeat is also a victory, and I can picture him waving his scarf as he did when they last won, and we celebrated with his friend who now pores over the old French grammar books—easy to read, easy to use.

I find happiness on every corner, and I understand that something is shifting, even if I don't know why.

I fly west and settle in for a fortnight in the house of mosaics, where Pearl the sleek spaniel is like a comforting seal. From time to time, I check on this year's falcons in Melbourne—there is a drama unfolding because the original father has been chased away by a younger interloper. Will this new father bird be able to care for the young, or will the mother have to manage alone? Why would a bird want the responsibility of another falcon's offspring? The websites are abuzz.

I go to the Indian Ocean each day, its salty bite a comfort. There are no seahorses for me to observe, but I think of my little friend and how he wriggled and wriggled for life. Dad is stilling. I can feel it. Sometimes it makes me want to thrash and move and wriggle harder—for life, for time, for more. A small plane flies low overhead one morning as I'm swimming, and I mistake its shadow on the white sand for a vast blurred bird. My heart beats fast, but when I surface, the plane is already far ahead of me, and in its wake there are only gulls, squawking that they too are important, they too are here.

But my main focus is Dad. He is struggling. His weight has dropped and he can't be tempted with anything, not even wine or Les's scones, so I meet with a palliative care team. They listen intently to me and to Dad.

The nurse pats my hand, telling me it's hard to grasp that Dad has a lot to live *with* now, but little to live *for*—except the family, of course, and it is our job to make it easy for him to let go.

We talk practicalities. They arrange to have an air mattress on his bed, so he won't get bedsores. It's squeaky, he tells me. Crinkly under his back. Like sleeping on newspapers.

'But I'll get used to it, honey.'

The palliative team talk with him about end of life. He is ready. He knows the celebrant he wants for his funeral and insists it be short. Preferably no longer than thirty minutes, he writes in a note to Justin. He knows what care he will and will not countenance. On the day I'm leaving, he is clear of eye and mind, but we're both flat, speaking in near-whispers.

'It will come, darling,' he says. 'What can you expect? I never thought I'd make it to ninety.'

'Are you frightened?' I ask, holding his tiny hand, so like the claw of a peregrine chick.

'No, darling. No. I'm just weary.'

He kisses my hand. I stroke his forehead, telling him I'll be back in four weeks. He says that will be good. I can come sooner, I say, but he just says no, that's fine. I tuck his sheet up around his neck, then the white cotton blanket, and then the navy-and-cream bedspread I'd found after so much searching. It had to be right. It had to be perfect. As though a bedspread could guard him from those winged shadows.

And yet, as I look around his room, with the lamps glowing softly and the roses and lavender in little vases, I know it matters that those watery, itchy eyes of his should be able to fall on some islands of beauty.

Lying on his side, he is barely visible above the bedclothes. He's like a seahorse, I see when I look again, his body curled in, his legs drawn up, curved like a tail.

How do I leave? Why?

Cursing myself, calling myself a bad daughter, I farewell carers and kitchen staff and residents as I make my way to the entrance where Bob is waiting to visit his wife in the dementia section. He says I'm a good daughter, and then I do cry. Sonia is there. I tell her I feel I'm deserting Dad. We cry together. I cry when I hug Justin. I cry on the plane. They are tears that need to fall. Sometimes falling is vital.

At home, I try to settle. Dad is still living, not dying; still defiantly in life. When people say it's not much of an existence, I say they don't know him. He is interested. He is curious. He remembers everything.

'What book are you reading on the balcony with the girls?'

'Did the voice job eventuate?'

'Have you seen your grumpy octopus again?'

My job now is to bring him stories. It's a reversal from six months ago, when he was the teller of tales. I go out with my eyes wide, hunting like a peregrine for morsels to enliven him. He is making me see the world anew.

Walking along a harbour path, I notice a circle of six people standing under a she-oak, their heads tipped back, staring into the branches. As I get closer, I begin to tiptoe. No one moves. There is something reverent about the hushed stillness. I stop a few feet from a woman in a hooded black sweatshirt and look up. Squinting into the shadows, I spot them: two wide-eyed tawny frogmouth chicks, peering down from beneath the fluff of their mother's wings. We humans don't move. In thrall, we barely breathe. The parent bird blinks slowly from under her outrageous eyelashes, content with her godlike status.

I describe the scene to Dad—it was like we were in church, I say—and he tells me he used to call them mopokes. For days afterwards, he will inquire about their progress. Are they fattening? Flying? Growing? Are they safe from cats?

'Your mum loved "The Owl and the Pussy-cat",' he says.

One night, when he doesn't pick up his phone, I call the nurse, asking her to check on him. Her name is Yvonne. She's from Argentina. She takes the phone with her, saying she was only in his room about fifteen minutes ago but she's happy to visit him again. I'm always happy to see him, she says.

'Hello, Yvonne,' I hear him say. 'Two visits tonight? Aren't I lucky?' He's always lucky.

Yvonne tells him I'm on the phone, worrying.

He laughs. 'She worries too much, that one. Tell her I'm fine.'

Yvonne asks if he needs anything.

'Not a thing, now you've been in,' he says, and I hear him thanking her as she leaves.

'He's special, your dad,' Yvonne says. 'It's a privilege to care for him.'

I assume she says this to everyone, but she goes on to tell me how he tries to remember the names and family stories of every carer, and thanks everyone for every small thing; that he is a gentleman and a gentle man.

It occurs to me that Dad is not just living, but teaching; that his life, the tiny flame of it, is still productive and useful. Like an irreverent, emaciated buddha, he's showing me—and others—what acceptance and gratitude look like.

There's nothing holy about Dad, but for me there's something sacred now. I flick through photographs I took on my last visit. In one of them, he seems lit from within. There's a purity about him; he's pared to the bone, and not just physically. Oh, he still gets cranky and frustrated, and he would kill for a drag or two on a gasper, but as the oxygen machine pumps away, and he lies there, a child-sized shape in his single bed, I stare into the photograph. The white cotton sheet over his bony body reminds me of the folds of marble in those sculptures of ecstatic saints in Roman churches.

The lucky man is ready, but not finished. His flame, like the one on the shrine I made for Peter, burns steady and clear.

repair

1. restore to good condition after damage or wear

Once, I watched an art restorer tending to a still life of full-blown roses. It was not a masterpiece, but she took such care, dabbing with her cotton bud while speaking of the privilege of putting damage to rights. It has something of the devotional about it, she whispered. I thought of Peter repairing that jug, and Dad under the bonnet of his Falcon. Tinkering, he called it, but it was restoration.

2. renovate or mend by replacing or fixing parts or by compensating for loss or exhaustion

For years, Dad would head off with fellow Rotarians to mend fences for widows. To ten-year-old me, such tasks seemed pointless, but when my heart—and my fence—got broken,

I understood such acts for what they were: humble attempts to compensate for life's brokenness.

3. *set right or make amends for (loss, wrong, error etc.)*

The French word for 'repair' is *réparer*. It suggests reparation. I prefer it. In my head, I hear the word 'amends'.

repair
a widow's definition

'Do you think you will find someone else?'
People are, I guess, asking if I want to *re-pair*.

Sometimes, on a hot day, I lie down among the angophoras with their twisting trunks and peeling bark and close my eyes, listening as sap rises and tiny creatures rustle, and there's a charge, a shiver through my body and into the earth, and the birds don't ask questions, just as the fish don't comment when I'm held by warm currents, limbs loose, open to the sky. In those moments, the someone else I find is myself.

I don't know what *repair* looks like, but something at the edge of my vision tells me Dad is teaching me about that, too.

Still life with skeleton, shell and nest

IT'S THE FIRST day of summer; nine months exactly since I flew across the border with my sisters. The water in the harbour is cool silk, the air is soft and moist, the latest falcon chicks have fledged and flown, winging out from their impossible height without a backward glance, but something niggles. We received an email from the nursing staff last night warning families that Covid is on the rise again. Not that, I pray, as I float on my back looking into an untroubled sky. Please, not that.

A single crow flies west, its voice harsh. *Aaaaark.*

Back home, I wait to call Dad. I'm due to fly over on Sunday—three more sleeps. I try to work, but my brain is like a disco. Since the hospital episode, whenever I get anxious, I experience spot headaches and fizzy buzzing sensations above my left and right ears. The neurologist insists they're stress, but that doesn't quiet them, and from the amount of activity this morning, I'm clearly wired. My seahorses are in danger of frying.

Justin advises me not to panic, he's close by, but also tells me they now have additional palliative medications handy, and Dad has instructed the staff that he's not to be taken to hospital if things worsen. He has never refused this before.

I roam my flat like a caged creature, eventually deciding that instead of putting up Christmas decorations, I will make a new still life. I nestle a seahorse skeleton inside the tiny nest I almost stepped on last week. It's an irregular bowl made of fibres and wisps of cobweb. Perhaps it belonged to a willie wagtail, though it's rare to see those impudent black-and-white tricksters here. Whoever made it, it was once a home. The seahorse was once alive.

These two, just like the final object I'm about to place next to them, have undergone changes—from life to death, full to empty. The matchbox is beige and brown, battered and stained. On its surface, an abstracted sun rises over the curve of a horizon. The offing. Above that image is the name of the place from which I souvenired it, three decades ago. *Windows on the World.*

Most visitors won't notice this arrangement. It's on a side table by the bathroom door; made for my eyes. Few will remember the name on the matchbook, so hopefully it can't cause distress. It will just be a quaint memento of another time. I mean, a matchbook in a restaurant—can you imagine? Smoking encouraged at dining tables? Bizarre, no?

But this oddity is precious. On the reverse is the address.

107th floor
New York World Trade Center

Peter and I went there for a drink. In the clouds, we clinked glasses, telling each other this must be how birds felt. What must it do to you, to soar at such heights? we wondered. Maybe birds are gods, I said.

'I'll take Manhattan,' Peter replied.

Years later, they did. All those people, all that life, falling to earth.

I step back from the still life, catching sight of a lorikeet as it flits, green and red, from branch to branch of the eucalypt. Did Peter fall, like a tree in a forest? Where will I be when my time comes?

And Dad? He's getting tinier and sleeping longer, barely able to raise his head, panting and gasping for air, but here. No more nine-letter words, but here. Still talking on the phone each day, though for less and less time. Still here.

I call repeatedly, but he doesn't answer, so I join the others on our balconies for Quiet Reading, though I can't make out a word of my book. I watch magpies in Lisa's birdbath. My kookaburra visits but doesn't stay. Marauding cockatoos career down onto Margie's balcony. Leaves rustle. My stomach churns, rumbles, rolls. Finally, we pack up and farewell each other. They wish me safe travels for Sunday, but I've a sense now that I will go before then. Fran says she will check on my place. She has my key and she has my back.

Inside, I tap Dad's number, and this time he answers. It takes ages to get the phone to his ear as he pants and strains. It feels cruel to have disturbed him.

'Hi, honey,' he manages, between ragged breaths.

I tell him I won't keep him, that I can hear he's struggling, can hear the oxygen machine, and for the first time he agrees.

'Don't worry, sweetheart,' he manages. 'Ah . . . Ah . . . Thanks for calling.' I want to tell him not to waste energy on thanks, but he continues. 'Love you, darling.'

He coughs. He gasps. He wheezes. I end the call, and in the silence, as his words reverberate, it's clear to me that we won't speak on the phone again.

Justin visits that evening and reports that Dad is 'pretty rough'. Like his father, he has understatement down to an art. I say I'll decide in the morning, but I know I will go. I manage a couple of hours' sleep, but my head is ticking and needling.

I rise before the birds and hustle: washing, cleaning, packing, sending texts and emails. I get a seat on the three o'clock flight, which will have me on the ground in Perth by five. My writer friend of the cloud-covered book has just completed cancer treatment but insists on driving me to the airport. She gives me dark chocolate and we hug. The plane is late, then on time, then early. Finally, I'm above a sea of cloud, winging west.

Winging it is what we say we're doing when we're improvising, both in the theatre and in life. It comes from a time when understudies would wait in the wings—the areas at the sides of the stage—studying the action in case they might have to perform.

This whole year has been improvised. There has been no script, and we've all played whatever role was presented to us. I suppose Dad has been the director, but his touch has been so light that we've felt we made our own choices. Now, though, I know I'm approaching the end of the fifth act.

Chaplain Campbell and his glamorous wife collect me at the airport. We speed down the freeway, them in Christmas party finery, doing their best to distract me as shadows lengthen. Dad's facility is closed when we arrive. A Christmas tree greets me in the foyer after Campbell opens the door. I wheel my suitcase around the holly-decked halls, glad not to see any residents. At door thirty-eight, I knock, then enter. My brothers stand on either side of Dad's bed, both in navy T-shirts and jeans. It's only when I see them that the world shifts back onto its axis.

'Look who's here, Dad,' Brett says. 'It's Ailsa.'

Dad lifts up in the bed, his eyes flicking open, and for a nanosecond I think he's normal. But his eyes close before I register what's happening.

'That's the biggest reaction we've seen,' Brett says quietly.

I go over to the bed and stroke his forehead, where Brett's hand has been. The brothers give me space. Dad's oxygen machine is working, and the prongs are in place in his nose, but his mouth is open so wide that it's like looking deep inside a hungry hatchling's beak. I tell him it's me. I say my name. I say I'm sorry he is struggling. His eyelids flutter and his arm twitches, but there's no way to know if he can hear, though Justin tells me the nurses say he can.

I was ready for his body to be wasted and his breath to be agony, but I hadn't considered that his mind—brain, spirit, what?—would already be taken by the morphine. I'm reeling, maybe not quite here yet. I've come nearly 4000 kilometres as the crow flies, and I'm not sure where to put myself. The brothers suggest that maybe we should get some food, but I say I'd like to sit a while, so they hug me and go.

The oxygen machine makes its usual *dah-dum, thump, thump.* I close the curtains against the coming night, and switch on the lamps I bought five months ago. The room glows. The noticeboard has the same photos and postcards I pinned on it back then. *Always Look on the Bright Side of Life*, I read, in big white letters on black. Sitting in Dad's navy recliner, holding his hand, I can't stop the earworm of the lyrics to that song.

The machine pumps on. Shifting position slowly so as not to disturb him, I study his profile. Oxygen goes into his nose through the prongs, but he seems to be breathing through his gaping mouth. The morphine must have relaxed his lungs and jaw muscles, along with his brain. Is he relaxed? His right hand tightens around mine, and his left clutches his leg. His fingers wrap right around it; he has his thighbone in a vice-like grip. I try to loosen it without letting go his right hand, but it's impossible. How can he have such strength? And why hurt his leg like that?

I whisper to him to relax, to let go, but this is not Disneyland and he holds and holds and I long for him to release himself from himself. Then, from the dark pool of long ago, my hippocampi drag up a memory, and I recall that prayer we were instructed to recite as children.

God grant us the grace of a peaceful death.

Back then, those words had no significance to kids in oversized hand-me-down uniforms. Now, it seems like the best prayer I could make for Dad. Perhaps it's the best prayer for everyone.

His left hand waves, as though he's conducting an orchestra. Is he dreaming or trying to communicate? I tell him it's alright, even though I have no idea what I mean. His right hand still holds mine, which once held a seahorse and before that held Peter's, and when it was very small, it held my father's big hand, and my mother's hand, which was the shape that my little hand grew into . . .

On my wrist, the word *HOPE* catches the light.

Three hours pass, measured by the rhythmic thump of the machine. From time to time I speak into the silence, telling

313

him I'm here. I whisper the first words I ever uttered—*Dad, Dad, Dad*—and tell him I love him. Anything else seems like a violation. He is in between now. He's not living. He has begun the work of dying.

The air mattress squeaks and wheezes when staff come to turn him. He is resting comfortably, a nurse tells me, and I want to know how she knows. One carer, Ron, is particularly gentle. He tells Dad he will shave him because I am here, and then he shows me how to wet Dad's mouth, using cubes of blue sponge on skewers. They look like lollies. I dip them in water, squeeze, and touch them to his dry lips and inside his hungry-hatchling mouth. His head strains, and I'm sure his body tilts ever so slightly towards me. Dip, squeeze, and dab to moisten.

The brothers return, and Brett prepares to settle into the navy recliner. He will stay, keeping vigil overnight. Justin and I leave him and walk the silent corridors. I've never been here this late. The place is a warm burrow, with a reassuring smell of leftover roast and cleaning fluid. For the first time ever, the word 'home' doesn't seem like a cruel joke. The silence is close and intimate, as though we are inside a creature that is breathing us towards the door. Even the budgerigars are tucked under their blanket. *Silent night*, I want to hum. Christmas decorations twinkle. *Holy night.*

Next morning, Justin and I arrive at seven. Brett reports there was no drama in the night, and Dad is still here, head back, skin taut, mouth agape, being breathed by the machine. Brett must head home to the bush but will return tomorrow. Justin and I are given tea and toast with peanut butter by the carers. We settle in; Justin scans Dad's newspaper and I read from a collection of poems I found at my digs. An hour passes.

I sneak glimpses of Dad—his cheeks still have a hint of colour, but his skin is patchworked with dry white flakes. There are two furrows between his brows, and I can't decide whether he looks worried or melancholy. It's impossible to tell with his mouth open in what looks like a permanent scream.

I sneak glimpses of my brother. Justin is sixteen years my junior but much steadier and calmer. For him, this death will be the end of years of quiet mateship. Well, I have no idea what it will be. We are four very different people, Dad's children, and I should not assume anything. But we will all be altered, like those objects I placed in my still life two days ago—objects that will probably outlive us all, like the milk jug that has survived generations of my clan; like scissors and tweezers, quotidian things that will remain long after I stop growing hair and nails; like soup ladles and coffee mugs that will be useful when I've burned to cinders and risen into the sky as smoke.

The feathered thing hovers. I swear I can feel the breath of its wings flapping, but then realise that it is, of course, the air conditioning that Jenn mended.

Justin heads off to do the weekend work of parenting. We've agreed I will stay with Dad until after dinner, when Justin will come and sleep over. I listen to the machine; then listen closely to the mattress making small squeaks; then listen to the scrabbling feet of a crow outside the thick glass door, and the *chortle-ortle-ortle* of a magpie that comes hopping. I'm offered tea, and more toast, cakes, sweets. Carers change his position again, and I leave the room to give them space. When they're done, the tall girl stands at Dad's door, her hand on her chest.

'Are you okay?' I ask. 'Did you hurt yourself?'

'Lifting your dad?' she says, and shakes her head. 'No. He just breaks me up. He's so polite. Even when we roll him over, he says thank you.'

She walks off, wiping away tears, and I'm touched, but also confused. Did he really speak? He has not said a word for fifteen hours, to my knowledge. I tidy away newspapers and clothes, telling him what I'm doing and why. I water the plant I sent him for Father's Day last year, and within an hour it has lifted its leaves. Instant revival, like a Lazarus. But that won't happen for Dad. He is like a winter leaf—all flesh gone, just a transparent skeleton.

I study the photos of his four children with our partners— two of them dead, from a haemorrhage and an aneurysm—and the barometer that I hung on the wall, right in Dad's eyeline. It has been with him for longer than any of us, more than seventy years, measuring pressure. He has known plenty of that.

Nurses come and go. They say Dad is now on 'comfort care', but he doesn't look comfortable with his mouth hanging open.

I worry the air mattress has deflated and he has been swallowed into it, because the bed's surface is totally flat. It's nine months to the day since I first visited, just before he got Covid, and I thought he was working to breathe then. But this . . . this straining . . .

Nine months.

Death, like birth, can be labour. Hard labour. He's working as hard as he has ever worked; straining to get down a tunnel or across a line or wherever the grace of a good death will take him.

My favourite nurse visits to check if he needs water or morphine, or if I need anything. It was she I called to say I was coming early. Her response was brief: 'This makes me happy.' Now, she strokes his hand, saying she is here and his daughter is here. She dabs his lips, telling me he's comfortable, so no extra morphine. Again I want to ask how they judge comfort, but say nothing. Though she's decades younger than me, I trust her.

She pats my shoulder, then whispers, 'There's a smell they get when they're near death. When I was cleaning his mouth, it was there.'

This intimate detail shocks me, and I remember Connaught, from back in the hospital last Christmas—surely that was not a year ago?—telling me death was interesting. I pray Dad is interested and not frightened, but to whom am I praying?

Judy visits. I leave her with Dad and walk the corridors, then return and we talk as I eat the lunch the carers bring, before leaving her again. It's afternoon and crows—or are they ravens, Dad?—line up on the roof on the other side of the courtyard. Bob tells me they had rats in the garden one year, and the crows feasted on their babies.

'Natural pest control,' he says. 'Chemical free.'

I pass a nativity scene and a spangled Christmas tree. The corridors are subdued for a Saturday, and one of the carers tells me everyone knows Dad is going.

I walk another circuit, and as I pass resident's door after resident's door, it hits me that death has visited all of these rooms, just as it visited Peter in our bedroom. It is always close, but we forget.

'I never thought something like that could happen here,' we keep hearing on news bulletins. 'Not here.'

Wherever we walk, a last breath has been expelled. All that holy ground underfoot. I see why we must fence in cemeteries: it's too much to comprehend that every piece of earth has death in it. Keep it inside its boundary and we can separate ourselves from it. It might be comforting to think we're all made of cells from stars, but the reverse of that idea is that we're all dust, and we constantly tread on families and friends, ghosts and ancestors, the old ones who were here long before we were even imagined.

Living requires us to forget that, at least for the most part, and to believe something truly crazy—that all the cups of tea and morning swims, small disappointments and triumphs, will go on forever.

When Judy leaves, I return to the blue chair. All is as it was. *Dah-dum, thump, thump. Dah-dum, thump, thump.* I squeeze, dab and moisten. I read a poem or two. Whisper that I love him. But mostly I'm silent.

Then my phone buzzes. It's my writer friend of the cloud book, sending a video of her husband, standing in the doorway to their garden, performing Louis Armstrong's 'Wonderful World' on his trumpet. I play it to Dad, very softly. I don't know if he hears, but his hand twitches and that's enough. I want him to know that others are holding their breath with him and for him.

My favourite nurse returns to tell me I need to give Dad an hour or two alone in case he wants to "go" without his children in the room. 'We will look after him, I promise,' she says. 'But you must give him some private time.'

I kiss his forehead, his hand, and enter the world of the living. I could make for the beach, or the shade of a tree, or Sonia's place, or even a chapel, but instead I head for the big shopping centre near his old place. I buy my groceries at his supermarket, wine from his bottle-o, a lotto ticket from his newsagent, and have a prescription filled at his chemist. The centre's lights are white neon, and it smells of fruit mince tarts, roasting poultry and adrenaline. Christmas shoppers wear antlers and Santa hats. They move fast, checking lists and talking on phones. I load up Dad's Falcon and drive down jacaranda-purple streets to my digs, where I unload, then lie down, gutted.

With nothing to do, minutes are like hours. If he were alive, now is the time I would call Peter to report to him about Dad. To make things a little more ordinary. Safe.

'Make a cup of tea,' he would tell me.

Dailiness. The thing we take for granted. That there is a person beside us at 2 a.m. to tell us to roll over, it will be alright in the morning. That there's someone who will agree that it matters when a misplaced comma sneaks into a finished work. That the choice of laundry detergent might be vital.

Dailiness. A phone call at the same time each afternoon, to hold the world from cracking apart.

I check the time again. He has had two hours, so I head back, to find there's no change.

I sit, watching the two of us reflected in the mirror. His hand lifts, as it did yesterday, but this time it's like a bird in flight. It settles onto the coverlet. It doesn't fall. It places itself. Or he places it. Is his mind telling him to lower it? Is his brain wriggling for life? Do his seahorses still swim?

Night has fallen. I close the curtains and open the poetry book. There is only the *dah-dum, thump, thump,* and I feel uncertain. I want him to know I'm here, but I don't want to chatter. We have nothing that needs to be said—all our talk is done, our feelings known—but I would hate for him to feel alone. He's not a man for prayers and piety, so I look for poems that are straightforward and without complications, like him.

I find the lyric to 'Danny Boy' and read it.

I give him some Emily Dickinson, pure and direct, because I do carry his heart, and I want him to know that hope can be a thing with feathers.

I whisper words from Peter's favourite Yeats: *I shall have some peace there, for peace comes dropping slow . . .*

I recite 'The Owl and the Pussy-cat'. I tell him I have loved it and I have loved him since before I had words. Then we sit in silence until Justin comes.

The nurse on duty speaks to us about Dad's oxygen machine. At this stage, she says, it is 'prolonging his life' and we should turn it off. I'm resistant. She's an agency nurse and doesn't know the discussions that have been had about his treatment—but on the other hand, is it cruel to keep it going? Is that what she means? Is he suffering?

No, she says. But it may not be helping him.

I'm trying to read between lines when Justin says we don't have to decide; that another few hours of oxygen won't hurt. I exhale. I am grateful that he has made the decision for no decision, which is a decision. The nurse agrees and leaves us. Justin tucks himself into the chair, reassuring me he will be fine, so I say goodnight to both of them and walk out into the silent holy night and drive Dad's car to my digs and make tea and sit very still.

No fuss, Dad has instructed us. He has arranged his funeral and spoken with his chosen celebrant.

The readiness is all, Hamlet said.

Dad wants things calm, and simple, so that's how I will be. I sip tea. I sit. I watch the clock tick to midnight, then shower off the nursing home scent. I read. I lie down. I whisper into the silence, something about how it will be alright, but my voice breaks. I make tea. I read. I check the time. I read some more. At 1 a.m., I turn out the light, and at some stage I sleep.

I wake, wide awake, at 4.15 a.m. There's a promise of light in the sky. I click the Wordle website and enter a word: ARISE. I could never get Dad to grasp how this puzzle worked. Too digital for him. I have three correct letters and two in the right position. I enter ADORE and watch all the squares turn green. Got it in two.

The phone rings. It's Justin.

'We won't have to make a decision about oxygen,' he says.

I'm at Dad's bedside twenty minutes later. He's not yet cold, but his skin is already like parchment, drawn too tight over his bones. His mouth is still wide open, like that baby bird, but the prongs have been taken from his nose and the machine is off. The silence is categorical.

I hug Justin. We stand. We sit. He tells the others, or maybe he already has. I don't know. I am watching my father, who has just made the crossing from *is* to *was*.

Justin must go to be with his family as sun begins to fill the courtyard and magpies wake. I say I will stay a little longer, maybe an hour. We hug. He leaves. I sit beside Dad, listening to the tick of the second hand on his watch. The universe rotates around this one small room and its deathly silence, too deep to fathom.

I recall a story he told about having to descend into the darkness of a well, going down down down on a swinging seat arrangement he'd rigged up, and feeling a snake, or was it two, swim between his legs, and knowing he should not be doing this, and that he could die alone, checking on a windmill and a well. He was a young man, in his twenties, wondering *if it be now*, and here he is, seventy years later.

Has he fallen, or has he flown? Did he rise into the stars, when the world was as inky and quiet as the grave?

Only this week, he asked a question I couldn't answer.

'Where do you think ideas come from, darling?'

I didn't know. He wondered if some of them come from outside of us. From somewhere else, if there is somewhere else.

The staff bring tea and ask if I'm okay. I stroke Dad's cooling forehead, stroke, stroke, and tell them I'm fine. I can hear him saying it. *I'm fine, honey. That's fine.*

Carer Ron, light of voice and step, arrives. 'Can I?' he asks. I nod and he goes to stand by Dad, stroking his jawline where he had shaved it yesterday.

'Goodbye,' he says. 'Goodbye. Goodbye. Goodbye.'

When he turns back to me, tears have dampened his mask. 'Thank you,' he says.

'No, Ron, thank you,' I say. 'My Dad loved you.'

'And I love her,' he manages to say, mixing the English pronouns as he always does, before hurrying from the room.

The funeral director will arrive soon, I'm told, so I decide to stay on. My seahorses wriggle, and I recall combing Mum's hair and tying the ribbon on her nightdress, but her room in the hospital was needed, so it wasn't possible to linger. Now, I sit. Dad gets colder and the world gets quieter. I hear a squeak from his mattress. Is something leaving? Soul? Spirit? Don't be daft.

Or be daft. What does it matter?

Chaplain Campbell comes. I ask him to say a prayer with me and he says of course, and so we speak softly, hoping Dad wouldn't mind.

Our Father, who art in heaven . . .

Leoni, on the front desk, told me she came to see Dad a couple of days ago and asked if she could pray with him. He said that would be 'fine', so she said her prayer. When I asked her what he did afterwards, she looked surprised. 'He said, "Amen",' she told me.

Campbell smiles when I tell him this. He was the last person to have a social chat with Dad before the morphine kicked in. He told Dad he'd like to say some prayers for him in the coming days if that would be okay. Dad thanked him, and said he'd take all the prayers Campbell could give.

I sit.

Ravens call from the roof opposite. Staff replace my tea cup.

It has been four hours.

I go over to the wheelie-walker and lift the lid. Lying there is a pack of cigarettes. I throw them in the bin. It's the first anger I've felt.

'Fuck off,' I say, then immediately, 'Sorry, Dad.'

I tidy his notepads, flipping through the pages. There are lists—of phone numbers and shopping and birthdays. The cursive letters become spidery and weak, as he did, but it's still his handwriting. I close my eyes, picturing it on birthday cards and letters, envelopes and bookplates. I open my eyes and put the lists in my bag, along with his mobile phone.

I sit.

I sit.

I could sit here forever, listening to raven rustlings in the courtyard.

I sit, knowing that huge chunks of my history have flown with him, and that I am now the oldest of my line, and that there is no one living who can remember me as a tiny, mewling creature.

I sit, remembering that his last words to me were that he loved me

I watch.

I sit.

This was what I couldn't do for Peter. This sitting, holding space and time, stretching and bending it as minutes tick by and the world is distant and close and intimate and vast; this honouring of the body as the spirit or soul or whatever leaves, and the hardworking vessel that's left behind bears witness to a life of struggle and joys, effort and delight. This sitting, this being together in death, as we were and were not in life, is infinitely precious. It is deep peace, yet also quotidian. It is normal, and human. It is repair.

A magpie scratches near the courtyard door. A raven lands on the guttering, then another joins it. They watch the magpie. I watch them. I watch Dad. I watch myself—my steady heartbeat, my quiet head. I breathe, easy and long, like I'm swimming in the dry western air. Swimming with Dad; out to the horizon, into the offing.

There's a knock on the interior door. The magpie flies away as the funeral directors arrive. They're soft-spoken but not pious, posing questions with polite efficiency. She asks if Dad is wearing any jewellery and I indicate his watch. She asks if I want it to go with him, and I say no, I'd like it, and so together we lift his tiny arm. His fingers have always been bent, but now they're stiffening. I wriggle them through the watchband, then allow myself a few seconds holding that cold bony hand in mine before replacing it on his chest.

She asks if I would like to stay while they transfer him onto the trolley, but I don't want to see him disturbed. I stroke his forehead and his wayward hair, his eyebrows, the furrows. I kiss his cheek and hands, blessing that hardworking body, giving thanks. It's as close as I will get to giving anyone the last rites, and I take my time.

Stroke. Stroke.

Outside his door, I slip his watch onto my wrist and clamp the metal band. Click.

Near the entrance, a nurse sees me and begins to weep. I stand with her, patting her back. A resident offers condolences. We hug. And then the trolley comes into view. Dad is in a bag made of velvety maroon. I fall in beside him. I remember walking with Peter down the aisle after we married, and standing beside his coffin at the funeral, stroking the midnight blue velvet shroud with its painted stars. Worlds are colliding, but that isn't the right word, is it, Pete? Is it, Dad? Come on. You're the word men. Colliding?

No. Worlds are meshing.

We step into daylight, and I know I will go to water. I need the glare of sand, the bite of salt and the buoyancy of blue. I need to be rinsed and held, sluiced, and to watch seabirds baring their breasts to the onshore winds.

But not yet.

They are closing the doors of the van. He is inside it, but he is also gone. As he's driven away, I wave in a kind of salute. On my left wrist, his watch ticks. It's 11.30 a.m.

A raven lifts off from the tree over the road, flapping slowly towards me. It dips, then rises and wheels overhead, a funeral bird silhouetted against the sun, before winging away towards the east. I blink, following it until it's just a speck, then turn to go. Dad's Falcon is waiting.

After . . .

VOICES DRIFT UP from the neighbour's garden.

All is calm, all is bright . . .

They are singing carols, now that Christmas lunch is turning into Christmas dinner and inhibitions have been released by a glass or three of fizz. The sun is dropping behind the city, making its way west, but it won't find the lucky man when it gets there.

My stripy towel and black togs hang over the balcony railing. I've plunged into the harbour twice today, stroking away the first layers of residual sorrow. Yuletide brine is always best, but this was something else. I splashed and somersaulted and kicked like crazy. No laps. No seriousness. All frolic. Perhaps the most potent way to claim life is to fritter it on play.

Another dip would be good, but for now all I want to do is doze like a Christmas puppy. I've been home two days. I keep falling asleep, then sleeping more. For the first time in years, I'm not on overnight alert. My phone is silent and so am I.

Slee-eep in heavenly peace . . .

We waited seventeen days for Dad's funeral so all the clan could be there. I mourned and read and grieved. Perth became a site of absence, just as Melbourne did after Peter died. Once again I had tasks—clearing out his room with Justin, writing words, finding gifts for the carers—and I gave myself to them, aware they were the last things I could do for the man who had loved me longer than anyone ever has.

I chose the outfit he would wear for his cremation. It was the same one he'd worn to lunch, just after the border opened—the shirt with navy palm trees and the captain's socks. I even ironed them. Then I swam. I walked and swam for days. I swam and I walked, and I missed him everywhere.

'I'm a distance man, I suppose,' he'd said one day when we were marvelling at his age. 'Never was a sprinter.'

Statisticians measure lives in length, but I prefer to measure by breadth and by depth. On those two, Dad excelled.

A willie wagtail came one morning to the mosaic house and battered at the window, its tiny body hitting the glass again and again, its beak pecking. Finally, not knowing what else to do, I whispered, 'Hello, Dad.' It stopped then and sat on the sill, flicking its tail from side to side. I knew the stories about the wagtail being a messenger from beyond, but I didn't know what to make of that little winged thing's insistence. I just thanked it; thanked Dad. I thanked him over and over as I went about those waiting days before the funeral. In the aqua blue and on his stretch of white sand, I gave thanks.

Afterwards, I thanked him as I flew east, away, home . . .

Is it home?

I still can't answer that, but I did know, then, that I longed for this nest, and I know that, for now, I am held, here, by the birds and the village, by the neighbours reading on their balconies, by the toadfish and the morning swimmers. I am held in this place that opened me to the world again.

For so long, I held back from happiness, not giving myself to it fully because Peter couldn't have it. But the watery winged life I have made would not have been possible if you had lived, Pete, so I have to say thank you. I am grateful to swim through these waters, and to wing it, up here in the gods. I am grateful to you for all you gave me. Including this life.

Life.

A four-letter word made of two vowels and two consonants, in perfect balance. It's the same in Italian: *vita* for vitality. *Vida* in Spanish. In your favourite language, Pete, it's only three letters . . . *la vie*. So much in so small a word.

And I can say it now. It is *belle*, this life I have because of you. Not more or less so than before, but yes, still beautiful, still star-studded and still wonder-filled, despite all that it throws at us and all we throw at it. Oh, life . . .

The carolling continues. Memories and birds flit about. The sky glows, and the eucalypt and palm trees rustle as lorikeets tussle with cockies, oblivious to the Santa hats below.

This place is home. Melbourne is home. Perth is, too. Maybe the whole world is home. Maybe there is no home. Maybe people are home.

So many maybes. So much not known.

I inspect the lines of my right palm—head, fate, heart and life. On that wrist is the bracelet inscribed with *HOPE*. On the left is the silver bangle Dad gave me two Christmases ago, and beside it his watch, ticking away the final moments of twilight. On my third finger is the remodelled ring, made of the one that came from Ning and Mum and my rings from Peter.

Closing my eyes, I see his freckled fingers sliding a plain gold band onto my fourth finger. I feel it hit my knuckle. I hear my whispered, 'Push,' and our laughter as it slid home. That memory is true.

I held a seahorse, its belly bursting with possibility. That, too, is true.

My kookaburra lands beside my towel. She eyes me off, her head tilting this way then that. She hops around to face the harbour, then flits across, landing on a branch of the eucalypt. She peers at me, at my saltwater hair and bare toes, shaped like my father's, then leans back and gurgles, her carolling throb as sacred as any hymn.

Season's greetings.

When she's done, she steps off her branch, and drops. I catch my breath, but then she flaps her wings, rising, and I exhale. In the silence left behind her, I curl and uncurl my fingers. Like seagrass fronds moving with the tide, they're wriggling for life.

acknowledgement

1   *the act or an instance of acknowledging*

2   *(a) a thing given or done in return for a service etc.*

     (b) a letter confirming receipt of something

3   *(usu. in pl.) an author's statement of indebtedness to others*

—PAGE 12 OF PETER'S OXFORD ENGLISH REFERENCE DICTIONARY

Thank you . . .

To everyone who appears in the book. I treasure your stories.

To my friends who listened and encouraged me for years as I gnashed teeth.

To Tim Baker (then editor of *Slow Living*) and Ashley Hay (then editor of *Griffith Review*). Your belief was a gift. Fragments of work you commissioned appear in the text.

To those who read my early fumblings—Tony Doherty, Susan Hamilton, Vicki Hastrich and Keith Robinson—for your generosity and spine-stiffening.

To Grace Heifetz at Left Bank Literary, for making me believe. And for irises.

To the Allen & Unwin team: Angela Handley for peregrine-eyed oversight; Genevieve Buzo, Christa Munns, Ali Moffatt and Sarah Barrett for care and encouragement; and Christa Moffitt for the perfect cover. I wish I could show it to those who've flown.

To Ali Lavau. Oh! Your insight and precision. Your eyes and heart.

To the incomparable Jane Palfreyman. Cheer, cheer! Your 'yes' meant—and will always mean—everything.

To Charlotte Wood for clear-eyed, rock-solid friendship and support.

To Peter's family, for their trust.

To my beloved siblings. Deep gratitude for your acceptance of me telling our story. Each of you could write a book, so it means the world that you allow this one to live.

And of course, to Mum, Dad and Peter.

With love . . .